I'm Already Disturbed Please Come In

PARASITES, SOCIAL MEDIA AND OTHER PLANETARY DISTURBANCES (A MEMOIR, OF SORTS)

GABRIELLE GLANCY

Oneiric Press

Book Layout ©2014 BookDesignTemplates.com
Author Photo by Meg Allen
Book Cover by Laura Duffy
Cover Photo by Bob Croslin
www.gabrielleglancy.com

I'm Already Disturbed Please Come In / Gabrielle Glancy. —1st ed.
ISBN 978-0-9912149-8-3

Illness is the night-side of life, a more onerous citizenship. Everyone who is born holds dual citizenship, in the kingdom of the well and in the kingdom of the sick. Although we all prefer to use only the good passport, sooner or later each of us is obliged, at least for a spell, to identify ourselves as citizens of that other place.

—Susan Sontag, *Illness as Metaphor*

Upon waking, he felt that he had received and lost an infinite thing, something he would not be able to recuperate or even glimpse, for the machinery of the world is too complex for the simplicity of men.

—Jorge Luis Borges, "Inferno, I, 32"

1.

One day, the day of the earliest snowstorm the Northeast had ever seen, October 29, 2011—I see myself watching myself collecting Facebook screen shots.

> We've been without power since Saturday afternoon and it may be out another week. It's snowed 10 or 12 inches, which didn't seem like it would be a big deal, but many of the trees were still in full leaf, so they collapsed everywhere; our apple tree was flattened -- splayed open like a smashed tulip -- and our big oak tree lost some huge branches . . .
>
> Like · Comment · about a minute ago · 👥

I start noticing what I am doing, where I am going and where I have been.

Images of balconies, fire escapes, trees, streets, streetlamps, cars—all covered with snow.

> First a few fluffy inches. Didn't look like it would stick. And then, denser flakes, more deliberate. Inches turned to feet.
>
> Like · Comment · 2 seconds ago · 👥

There's Nancy Boutelier—when did she move east again, anyway? —drinking her coffee on her back deck, Starbuck's paper cup in hand, capped, and coffee-stained.

coffee on the deck this morning... — in Northborough, MA.

Like · Comment · Share   👍 31 💬 12

All that white stuff on her picnic table.

Inches upon inches.

Is she sitting right in it?

Her pants must be getting wet.

Her baby palm has not yet been taken in for winter.

I am soon obsessed with Facebook images of trees in full leaf downed by the snow.

In fact, I notice I have started collecting them.

Like · Comment · Share

Like · Comment · Share

I feel for those trees.

Particularly Cliff's old apple—the only thing growing in his
Brooklyn courtyard—just in the process of giving up its leaves

when the heaviness came down—*splayed open like a smashed tu-lip.*

I grew up in New York City. Sometimes the snow comes early.

Buried cars, traffic-less streets—that quiet, quiet city, blanketed by snow, stopped dead in its tracks. I remember those days . . .

Here our weather is unseasonably warm—an even layer of warm fog. The fog is both inside of me and out. That's what it's like in my head when the feeling comes.

Snow was general all over Brooklyn . . . falling softly in the dark mutinous waves . . .

Like · Comment · a few seconds ago · 👤

And my mind, the part of it that brings photons into focus and finds the words to describe it, draws back, as if it's had enough for the day, I think I will close up shop now and take a rest.

2.

When I feel good, I tell the story of what happened.
When I can't do that, I facebook.

3.

"Are you all right? " Tali Zeck said to me last night about ten minutes into our session.

In the middle of explaining the quadratic formula, I started feeling strange.

"Negative b plus or minus the square root of b squared minus four a c all over two a," I repeated like a mantra as if the formula itself or the act of repeating it could keep me from passing out.

"You gotta keep saying it over and over," I explained to her. "Pretty soon, it'll become second nature and you can call it up anytime you need to use it."

"When *do* you need to use it?" she asked.

The tingling had started in my arms and I could feel my jaw tightening and my stomach beginning to get hard.

I pointed to the formula. Suddenly, the numbers and letters started running together and it was all just a big blur.

"Are you OK?" Tali asked me again.

"Yea, I feel a bit weird, though." I said. "I'll tell ya what. I'm gonna run to the bathroom for a minute, and then I'm gonna grab something to eat. I don't think I've eaten enough today."

Tali was polite but looked worried. I excused myself and made my way to the back of the café.

Thank God, Patrick, the manager of the Noe Valley Star-buck's, mops the bathroom every hour on the hour because, at moments such as this, all I want to do is lie down on the floor. And so, work clothes and all, that's exactly what I did.

This seemed to relieve the pressure in my stomach and bring the blood back to my head.

I knew I had only a few minutes to save face. More than that and Tali would start to worry. If she started to worry, she'd tell her mom and then her mom would start to worry. And that would be the end of me.

Getting kids into Harvard is not that easy. At the very least, you need to be wide-awake while you're doing it.

I knew I needed to get myself together fast.

And what would I tell Tali? How would I explain what was happening to me?

Thankfully, the feeling started to pass. Sounds became more distinct, my jaw loosened, and I was able to stand up and get my balance.

Just as I was coming out of the restroom, Pam, Tali's mom, was coming in.

"Hey, Pam," I said. "How ya doin'?"

"I'm good," she said. "How are you?"

"I was just getting myself a snack," I explained. "Hypoglyce-mic," I lied.

"Oh me, too!" Pam said. She seemed delighted. "Came with the change." She winked at me.

For the moment, I was in the clear.

4.

Clouds in cages?

Like · Comment · Share

I notice when I wake up I am not really awake for a long time. Sometimes it takes me two or three hours . . . and sometimes it doesn't quite happen at all.

5.

Let me ask You a question, he retorted, If I was supposed to be Baby Boba Fett, then why would I have all these pool floaties in my asshole?

Like · Comment

And even those obscure moments, those moments of "huh?"—I seem to want to record.

Someone, somewhere must be in on it. Even if I don't have a clue, someone must. It makes me feel there's a whole world out there, even if I can't be a part of it.

Before this strange—I don't know what you'd call it—state of things—I never bothered much with Facebook. In fact, I had judgments about people who did.

For the longest time, I had my original fifty-three friends and that was just fine.

I just couldn't see what all the hype was about. It felt like reliving the worst parts of high school, being old enough to know better and doing it anyhow.

Now it often seems it's the only thing I can do.

"Why do you think we walk our dogs?" My friend Erin says, trying to console me. "So they can lift their legs and leave their two cents on every bush between here and kingdom come. Then they walk around and smell the trees. It's like reading the newspaper. All the news of the day is written there. That's what Facebook is like," she said. "It's all right that you do it. We all do. It's like smelling the trees."

6.

Today I praise the renegade meditators who say they're as likely to bask in the sweetness of enlightenment while cooking a frozen burrito in a microwave under the fluorescent lights of a convenience store as they are when they're contemplating the Great Mystery on a straw mat in a remote mountain sanctuary. Rob Brezsny's Free Will Astrology

Like · Comment

I went to college with Rob Brezsny. I remember him with dreads down his back and a band of followers even then.

These days, I am so close to a state of nothingness, I feel like if I meditated, I'd just disappear.

It is like running through treacle. Is that the expression? No matter how fast I am going, I can't seem to pick up my legs.

After four miscarriages—I lost five babies in all, twins once—at the age of forty-seven, I adopted a child, my son Marco, from Guatemala. And then, two years later, I met Sudha, who had a son nine months older than mine. Now I have two sons and a young, very beautiful partner.

"Before this strange thing happened, I had more energy than all three of you put together," I tell her. But I'm not convinced she believes me.

A host of white umbrellas with light bulbs in them, hovering between two buildings . . .

Wall Photos
Back to Album · ö6"Art"obgn's Photos · ö6"Art"obgn's Page   Previous · Next

Like Comment

ö6"Art"obgn
Like · Comment · Share · July 2   Album: Wall Photos
                                                                          Shared with: Public
32 people like this.
24 shares   Download
                                                                          Report This Photo
Write a comment...

I think that about describes it—except some of my lights are out.

7.

A week after Sudha and I met, I landed in the emergency room for the first time.

Sudha texted me through the night.

"I'm with you in spirit," she wrote. "Hang in there. I know you will be okay."

But the third time I called her from the ER, just three weeks after our first date, she seemed skeptical, even a little annoyed.

"Does this happen to you often?" she said, as she signed me out and we headed back to my place.

Granted, it was two in the morning and she had to wake up Zane and drag him out in his pajamas.

"No," I said. "I mean yes. I mean, these days it does."

8.

A tiny image. Almost need a magnifying glass to see it.

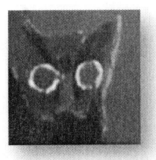

I click on it.

I feel like I look like this cat—sunken beneath my eyes.

9.

Cliff tells me he has not heard from our friend David for more than a week. He is worried about him.

"He may be too weak to answer the phone," he says. I understand this.

Sometimes when I speak, it seems as if my voice must traverse a long distance to come out of my mouth. It's down there somewhere; I can feel it. It's just that I have barely enough energy to pull it out.

David Rakoff is only forty-six. The last time I saw him in New York, he was full of the joys of life.

Sometimes life seems so random. Sometimes I think maybe I have cancer too.

10.

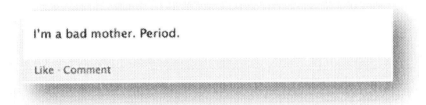

I'm a bad mother. Period.

Like · Comment

Why would you say such a thing? I'm embarrassed just reading it.

Although, lately, I kind of feel that way myself.

"Mommo," Marco said to me this morning when I took him out of his crib. "Are you still sick?"

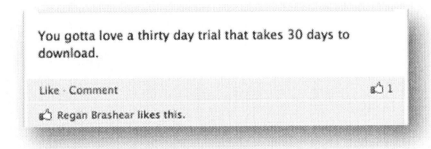

You gotta love a thirty day trial that takes 30 days to download.

Like · Comment   👍 1

👍 Regan Brashear likes this.

Sometimes I am too restless to think.

Writing is easy.
Just Open a Vein
And Bleed.

Like · Comment

Sometimes I am asleep and awake at the same time.

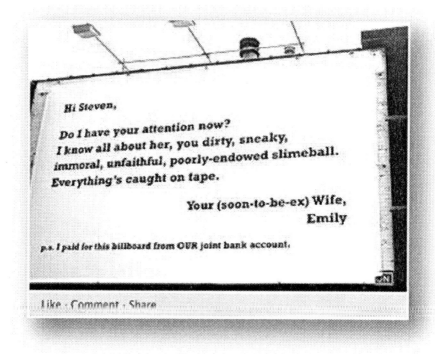

Then at bedtime, it's only a matter of slipping soundlessly back into the warm sea of hazy light I've been swimming in all day. Like a lumbering animal, a Grendal who retreats from all the carousing and endless detail, I am done feeling left out of the world.

11.

From the brackish waters of my afternoon nap to the primordial soup that is Facebook.

Weird Creatures Found In Ocean Muck Still 'Breathing' After 86 Million Years
www.huffingtonpost.com

Breaking News and Opinion on The Huffington Post
www.huffingtonpost.com

Breaking News and Opinion

Like · Comment · Share

At first glance, there doesn't appear to be much happening in the mud buried 30 meters below the Pacific Ocean sea floor. But this ancient muck, which hasn't had a fresh shot of food or sunlight since the days of the dinosaurs, still harbors life--if just barely.

It's the "if just barely" I relate to.

Except for the fact that at any given moment I may not be able to maintain consciousness, I'm in one of those in-between times in life, I think to myself, when it feels like nothing is really happening. No big dramas. Nothing to write home about.

My parents, god bless them, are still alive. In their eighties, they are drifting downstream, slowly, almost perceptibly—their voices, like cobwebs among the swaying branches, seem ever more distant, further away.

My young sons, they are growing. Sometimes, when I stand above their sleeping, pajama-clad bodies, it seems to be happening in front of my eyes.

12.

did you know?

In 1500s, Mapuche warrior Galvarino had both hands cut off as punishment for defying the Spanish. He returned home, raised an army and fought the Spanish with blades tied to the stubs of his arms.

ou-kno.tumblr.com

Like Comment

Seventh Generation Fund for Indian Development
Self-determination – for our peoples, for our cultures, for our homelands ... for the generations to come.

Like · Comment · Share · June 27

Album: Wall Photos
Shared with: Public

Download
Report This Photo

429 people like this.

1,036 shares

Risa Rodgers badass warrior-yah! showed them, hmm.
June 27 at 5:49pm · Like

My friend Regan, who's working on a documentary about "able-ism," tells me the story of a friend of hers who was in a car accident that left him paralyzed. His car fell two hundred feet down a ravine. He saw it coming; he knew it was an accident he

21

could not prevent; his car would be thrown off the cliff. And, of course, that's exactly what happened. In fact, it was a miracle he survived. In a wheelchair now, he still teaches at MIT. Apparently, the whole way down he was coming up with Plan B.

I understand this.

My Plan B?

If I lost my arms, I'd write with my feet. If I lost my feet, I'd write with my tongue. If I were blind, I'd write in Braille and listen to music all day long. If I lost my hair, I'd tattoo a line of Rumi on my head. If I were deaf, I'd paint. If I were paralyzed, I'd write with my eyes. And so on.

But losing consciousness? It's hard to work around that one.

"A weaker person would already be dead, " I tell myself.

"You gotta keep fighting until you find out what's wrong," my eighty-four-year-old mother tells me. Sometimes I feel like a warrior and sometimes I feel like that weird creature found at the bottom of the ocean.

13.

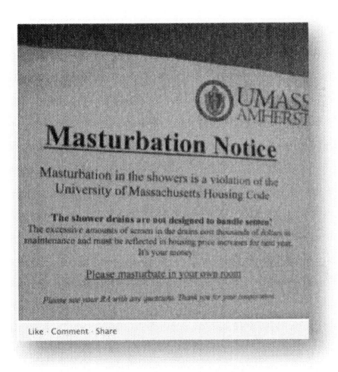

I do masturbate in my own room. Often. And I seem to levitate while I'm doing it. Honestly, sometimes my body feels like it is lifting off the bed.

And sometimes when I facebook, I draw the curtains and look over my shoulder, as if I'm afraid to be caught in the act.

14.

"Wanna Occupy with me?" Caitlin, my former girlfriend, asks. She tags me in her plea for people to "like" *Occupy Consciousness.*

"I'm not sure I can occupy anything right now," I tell her, but I check out the site.

I believe another world *is* possible, and for a moment, I consider joining the movement. My grandmother marched shoulder-to-shoulder with John Reed and Emma Goldman, stood up for civil rights, and would have occupied her heart out given half a chance.

Ironically, when I dated Caitlin, she was herself suffering from a mysterious illness that no one could diagnose. She was tired all the time and losing her hair.

"Every time I take a shower," she cried, "clumpfuls come out in my hand."

At the time—I suppose because I am twenty years older than she is and I didn't yet have a trace of the condition that had come to *preoccupy* me—I am embarrassed to say, I had very little sympathy for her.

Caitlin slept at the very edge of the bed with earplugs in her ears and a pillow over her head so as not to allow even a breath to disturb her. In the six months we dated, she only slept at my house twice. The one time I slept at her house, I left at two in the morning, hurt and confused, because she would not let me touch her. She had to be asleep by nine, she told me. She had to take her supplements, put on her nightcap (she really did wear a hat—a little red knitted hat with a pom-pom hanging off it), and drink the sleep potion her Choctaw medicine woman had given her. I got tired of soundlessly occupying the loveless space way over on my side of the bed and decided to leave.

As I was putting on my clothes, Caitlin woke for an instant, poked her head out of the covers and managed to squeeze out, "I love you but I gotta sleep. I'll call ya in the morning."

I thought she was making the whole thing up.

You'reanabsolutelybeautifuljuicyvibrantyoungtwentyeightyearoldthing! I texted her the next day.

"Thanks, honey," she said.

What I really meant was: "How can someone as young as you always be so tired?"

15.

Look. There's RFK.

Suddenly I feel a surge of moral fortitude. In fact, for a moment, I feel uplifted.

Square jaw, heavy-lidded bright blue eyes, that shock of straw-colored hair. He looks a lot like his mother. And so alive in this picture.

How old *was* he when he got shot? He couldn't have been more than thirty-five.

Sometimes the littlest things *do* make a difference—though I don't have a lot of energy at the moment to stand up for my ideals or to stand up at all, for that matter. I'm glad I "joined" *Occupy Consciousness*. I might as well show my solidarity, even if I can't pitch my tent at city hall.

16.

Dr. J, my GP, is close to seven feet tall. He looks like Karim Abdul Jabar in a lab coat. He has to lower his head when he walks into the office. He does it shyly, almost apologetically, as he reaches out to shake my hand. I find it very endearing. He told me he's originally from Jamaica—even though he was raised by his mother in Birmingham, England, went to medical school at the University of Chicago, and, recently, when I asked, he told me he had just turned thirty-two.

Under normal circumstances, I visit Dr. J as often as seems justifiable.

He's very gentle and sweet and seems to take a real interest in me, not in my health necessarily, but in whatever I'm up to at the time. I share all my new ideas with him. He's very receptive and encouraging. Like when I tried to start something called Townsquare.com—years before Facebook showed its face, as it were—I told Dr. J all about it.

I actually brought my laptop into Dr. J's office so I could show him what I had been working on.

"The thing is," I told him, "You can leave a trace of where you've been on the Internet like the tail of a meteor, a fine mist, the scent of yourself"—I was waxing poetic, *wherever you go, there you are*—"with a profile, (much like the one Facebook uses now), embedded underneath, so you can actually run into people you know, or meet friends of friends, just by shopping at Sears."

He looked impressed.

"That's interesting," he said, bending down to take a look at my beta. "*Very* interesting. Well, Miss Glancy, I guess we should go."

I had been in there almost an hour.

"It's always good to see you," he said, extending his huge hand out to mine.

"You, too, Dr. J!"

"And good luck with everything!"

We shook hands and I was off until the next time I noticed something slightly amiss in my general state of health or until I invented something else I wanted to share with him.

This visit was different. I was really sick and had come to Dr. J, sort of as a last resort. In fact, for months, I had been avoiding Dr. J completely. I thought if I ignored my symptoms, they would pass. I tried to convince myself that what was happening to me wasn't real, that it was all in my head.

I never like to visit Dr. J when I'm really sick. It takes all the fun out of it.

But this time, I'd already been in the ER twice and had been harboring this mysterious illness for upwards of nine months.

"There's something eating me from the inside," I told Dr. J. His smooth brow furrowed, his face very still and serious.

He was at his computer, reading last night's report.

"In the ER again?" he said.

I nodded.

"That's not good. Tell me your symptoms, Miss Glancy. How would you describe what's wrong with you?"

"It's like I have energy somewhere in my body, and then it gets taken away. I don't know how else to explain it."

"Hmmm," Dr. J said. He looked genuinely concerned.

"And I have palpitations, constantly, all day long. My heart keeps beating strangely. Also, my head is foggy a lot of the time, like I have cotton balls in my head."

"Cotton balls?" he said.

"Like I think something, and then it takes me a long time to remember what I just thought, if I can remember it at all. And it seems like my ability to speak goes way underground, so when I do want to speak my voice has to travel a long distance to break the surface and make a sound."

"Hmmm," Dr. J said. "Is that what landed you in the ER?"

"When I have an attack, it just gets more extreme."

"Oh, I see," he said. "What happens then?"

"My stomach blows up into a hard balloon, and I can't breathe. It's like my stomach takes up all the room my lungs are supposed to fill, and there's no room for any air to go in. And then, I guess because I'm not breathing well, I start to pass out. Could it be stomach cancer?" I ask him. "An aneurism?"

We decided to look it up.

Dr. J turned his screen around and googled aneurism just as I would do if I were on my computer at home. Then he got up and graciously motioned me to sit down on his rolling stool while he stood behind me, bending over.

There was a picture of a vein that looked like it had a balloon inside.

"They can burst, " Dr. J said. "That's the danger."

Indeed, I did have a feeling a vein or artery or some kind of tube had lost its elasticity and expanded beyond repair somewhere in my midsection.

"That scares me," I said.

"Or, Miss Glancy," Dr. J suggested, "You might have colonic ischemia."

"Oh my God, that sounds terrible," I said, really starting to worry. "What is that?"

"It's a constriction of blood vessels to your intestines," he said. "It sounds like something is stopping your stomach from getting enough blood."

"It feels that way," I said. "How would we know if that's what I have?"

"It's hard to diagnose," Dr. J said. "And it would be unlikely for you to get it at your age. It tends to hit people much older than you. People in their seventies. You do have high cholesterol, though."

"I know," I said. "It runs in my family. What else could it be?"

Dr. J seemed stumped.

"It's a complex picture," he said. "Because it sounds like all your major organs are involved—your heart, your lungs, your stomach, and even your brain."

"Yes," I said. "That's right!"

I felt for a moment as if we had just discovered America!

"Okay, so what do we do now?"

"As I've told you, Miss Glancy, I really think you should schedule a colonoscopy so we can get a look inside. In fact, why don't we do a million-dollar work-up?"

"That sounds good," I said.

"I'll call in referrals. At the very least, it will help us rule things out."

Dr. J smiled, reached down to shake my hand and quietly, as if he were a mouse and not the giant he is, slipped out the door.

I sat for a while in the empty office, trying to gather enough strength to head to my car.

I found myself staring at the garbage can. I don't understand why they put them next to the patient's chair in all these offices. At the very least, it seems unsanitary. In any case, it's unpleasant and you have to look over the top of the garbage can to see your doctor.

While I was sitting there, the screensaver on Dr. J's computer came on. Soon rainbow-colored fish were bouncing from one end of the screen to the other as if the edges of the screen were the sides of an aquarium. Bubbles came out of their mouths and rose to the top of the screen.

17.

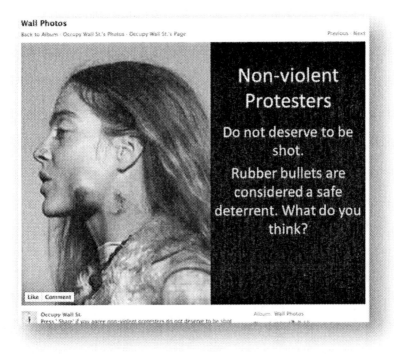

Non-violent Protesters

Do not deserve to be shot.

Rubber bullets are considered a safe deterrent. What do you think?

Like   Comment

Occupy Wall St.   Album Wall Photos
Press "Share" if you agree non-violent protesters do not deserve to be shot.

I stared at this image a long time.

What do I think?

I don't think rubber bullets are safe.

35

18.

Sometimes I feel invisible, even to myself. My pulse seems as big as the room, throbbing across my field of vision like the cursor on my screen. I feel like a huge throbbing animal, one big whale of a nerve like the mother tree in Avatar. Like the boundaries of my being have grown so thin and so vast, I am like an edgeless cloud or a jellyfish whose membrane stretches beyond the borders of this screen.

Even sleep seems too defined a state for me.

And yet, as muted as my perceptions sometimes are, especially when I am having an "episode," at other moments, it all seems too vivid.

I noticed the other day, for example, that I am acutely aware of changes in barometric pressure. The smallest fluctuation registers in me like an allergy. My sinuses become aroused as if they have just woken from a thousand-year sleep; my ears hum with the increase in humidity. You'd think I'd just dropped in from 30,000 feet. And the light. I see the difference. Sometimes it's got a peachy color in it that gets hazier and hazier as it goes up. And sometimes I can almost see particles of light flashing in front of my eyes. Like tiny golden arrows, they arc across the field of my vision, like my own private shooting stars.

Yesterday while I was taking a shower, there were thousands of them. Like little sparkling protozoans . . . it was like the northern lights inside my head, like aurora borealis.

"I think you should tell Dr. J," Sudha said. I could hear her nervousness.

Actually, I could tell she was beginning to think I was crazy.

So I emailed Dr. J and described the phenomenon to him.

I had already had a CT scan and everything looked normal.

"Let's get you tested for epilepsy," he said.

19.

The famous neurologist suggested I be put on a tilting table to see whether my "state" had an orthostatic component, which he said was typical of my condition.

"A tilting table?"

Dr. Dustal explained that in this particular test, they strap you to a table that revolves around an axis. The table then rises up, kind of levitates and tilts you at various angles to simulate the movement of rising or standing after you've been sitting down.

"Huh," I said. "I see."

Dr. Dustal had a ruddy complexion and straight extra-fine strawberry blond hair that seemed particularly susceptible to static electricity because it kind of stuck out to the sides, dustily, as if kicked up by the energy around his ears. He was a square man with a square head, and his tie had a very tight square knot, loosened at the neck. Head of neurology at Kaiser Lakeside, Dr. Dustal looked exactly like the 8 by 12 photo of him that hung alongside the photos of the other neurologists in the Kaiser Lakeside neurology waiting room. He was very enthusiastic and by all accounts had a winning reputation.

The examining room already seemed to be tilting as we spoke under the hum of the fluorescent lights above our heads. And Dr. Dustal grew dimmer at moments as if he were speaking to me from behind a piece of thick glass, like the cartoon version of himself, warped and warbled, not completely real.

Next Dr. Dustal ran his fingers down the outside of my legs.

"Can you feel that?" he said.

Of course I could. I wasn't numb. I just felt sick and as if I were always just a breath away from fainting!

"Hold your arms out to your sides," he said, "like an airplane."

I did what Dr. Dustal asked.

"Now bring the index finger of each hand up to touch your nose."

I did this too.

"Hmmm . . ." Dr. Dustal said. For a moment, he looked perplexed.

Then he asked me to describe my symptoms again.

"I'm going along relatively fine—I mean not a hundred percent—but okay enough, and then kind of out of nowhere, I begin to get this weird feeling, a heaviness and a floating at the same time. My jaw gets tight like it's wired shut. And my stomach starts to expand and get hard like a balloon blown up almost too much, like one of those exercise balls. I pointed to a bright purple ball in the corner of the room. Dr. Dustal looked at it for a minute and so did I. "Like that. And then—I don't know how to describe it—my consciousness starts to recede. It's almost happening now . . . Like everything slows . . . way . . . down . . . and gets fuzzy and far away. At the same time, my heart starts racing and beats strangely—like instead of going *ba-boom, ba-boom, ba-boom*, it goes, boom, *ba-boom, baboomboomboomboom-boomboomboom!*

" You know what I mean? I kind of go into a coma, but not really that extreme. I can't talk. I kind of can't move either."

As I was speaking, I noticed that Dr. Dustal seemed to be getting really excited. In fact, he looked as if he were jumping out of his skin.

He burst out: "You are a textbook case!"

He was beaming.

"Wait here," he said. "I have an article for you to read that describes exactly what you have."

In a flash, Dr. Dustal was gone.

By this time, I was tired. All the talking had exhausted me and I was trying not to go into the very state I had been describing to him.

I sat in the fluorescent light of the examining room examining the sensations I was feeling and not feeling inside a body that seemed to have become all brain. I felt like I was a walking sinus with little legs and arms that tingled from time to time when they encountered gravity or motion or any of the other laws of nature but my limbs were tiny and bug-like compared to the big head that housed my strange sensations.

"Here it is!" he said. He was absolutely beaming. "You can take it with you, if you like. I have other copies!"

He shook my hand, vigorously, and for a long time, as if to congratulate me.

"Thanks, Ms. Glancy," he said, and then, suddenly, he was gone.

Dr. Dustal's red face lingered, an afterimage on the eye, and seemed to hover there in the hazy ribbons of fluorescent light that hummed with their excited, staticky offering of luminescence.

Was he sunburnt, I wondered, drunk, or just really jazzed? His face was so red.

I was glad my condition excited him so much.

For a moment, it almost excited me—except that I felt so strange—in spite of the fact that I now had a name for what happened to me when I started losing it. In fact, far from comforted, I was calculating the distance between Dr. Dustal's office and the parking lot and hoping that I would make it without having to get any help.

I was already in the hospital, however, which was always a comfort. I always relaxed a little once we got to the hospital because I figured that, if I passed out, I was in the right place for it, and that someone could get me somewhere where theoretically I could get some help.

I sat for a while by myself in his tidy, sparkling, powder-blue and white Kaiser examining room.

No one came to find me, offered me a way out or further explanation.

Eventually, I unfolded the Xerox the famous neurologist had given me.

The article was entitled, "Neurocardiogenic Presyncope."

> Neurocardiogenic fainting usually occurs while standing. Emotional stress, stressful conditions and pain may trigger an episode, especially among the young (Shah, Gupta & Lokhandwala, 2003). The onset may be abrupt or associated with warning symptoms such as fatigue, weakness, nausea, sweating, pallor, visual disturbances, abdominal discomfort, headache, pins-and-needles, lightheadedness or vertigo (Deering, 2003). Presyncopal patients may also complain of palpitations, vomiting, disorientation, and difficulty speaking clearly or coherently (Grubb & McMann, 2001, p. 60.).

> Other symptoms that may present before a faint include feeling either warm or cold, tremors, yawning and having a bluish/purple or red coloring to the skin (Alboni, Brignole, Menozzi, Raviele, Del Rosso, Dinelli, Solano & Bottoni, 2001).

The doctor had said the words "neurocardiogenic presyncope" a few times during our meeting.

"Yep," he had said like a satisfied farmer, patting the paper. "That's exactly what you have!"

I folded the paper back up again and went wobblingly out to see if I could make it to my car.

Neurocardiogenic presyncope, it turns out, is just the fancy term for fainting.

20.

On my good days, the fog lifts somewhere between four and five-thirty p.m. For a moment, everything seems like it will be okay.

In the evening of one such day, I made the mistake of going dancing. I felt relatively stable. Sudha and Zane were away for the weekend, communing with the spirits at *Symbiosis*. I love to dance. It seemed like a good idea at the time.

At the last minute, I convinced my new friend, Edna, to go too.

"It'll be fun," I said. "A great place to meet people." Edna was single. "Very low key."

I arranged for Cara, my tenant, to babysit Marco. The year before Marco arrived, I built a cottage at the back of my property so I could rent it out to babysitters.

I polished my black cowboy boots—and though I felt a little weak—I thought the adventure would do me good.

The ride there was a little iffy. I had the precursor to the feeling that leads to the feeling—jittery and spaced out.

Edna was there when I arrived.

"You go," she said. "I'm just warming up to the idea."

So I grabbed Marguerite, one of my favorite dance partners, and took her for a spin.

"So where have *you* been?" she asked, flirtatiously.

"Oh, around," I said. "Busy."

"We've missed you."

"Aww, that's sweet. Gosh, I'm getting winded."

"Take it easy," she said. "Don't knock yourself out."

About halfway through the dance, I started seeing double.

"Wow," I said. "This one's fast."

She simply smiled.

"Whew," I said. "I think I gotta stop. I'm feel like I'm having a heart attack."

Now Marguerite looked perplexed and a little scared.

"You okay?" she said.

"Just a little out of shape."

"Okay," she said, squeezing my hand. "I'll catch you later."

"Girl, you can really move," Edna said, as I came off the dance floor.

My heart was racing and I couldn't catch my breath.

"Thanks," I said. "I was trying to impress you except I think I'm going to faint."

Edna looked startled.

"You look pale," she said. "You don't look good."

"I don't feel good. I need air. Let's go out on the balcony."

We pushed through the ticket line and out the double doors. I lowered my head to my knees to try to get the blood to my head.

Edna stood over me like a doting grandmother.

Just then, it started to drizzle.

"Maybe we should go inside?"

"Call 911," I said. "I'm losing it fast."

"911?" she said.

I passed her my phone.

Now it was really raining. Big drops were falling off my fore-head and into my eyes.

"Look up Cara—the babysitter. Call her and tell her she can sleep over; I may not be coming home."

Edna did exactly as I asked. She was the oldest of six kids from an Irish-Catholic family in Boston—and the only girl. She knew what to do in an emergency.

Next thing I knew, she was stuffing me into the back of an ambulance.

Thank God, I built that cottage on my property, I was thinking to myself.

I was always afraid Marco would see me die. That would be a terrible thing to happen to him. I adopted him from Guatemala. The least I could was survive his childhood.

As it was, twice already, he had ridden with me in the back of an ambulance. And once, the firemen took him up front.

When I rented the cottage in my backyard to Cara and Gabriel, I had no idea I was going to be so sick.

Lucky for me, though, Cara was in nursing school. She was always home studying for one exam or another when I needed her. Her father had been murdered when she was a kid and her mother had recently been diagnosed with MS so she had a deep empathy for my being sick and endless patience for letting me talk about it.

Edna came with me in the ambulance. I knew what was happening, but I was in that weird in-between state in which I'm there and not there all at the same time.

"You look great," one of the paramedics said to me, offhandedly, as he wrapped the blood- pressure cuff around my arm. "In fact, you look just fine!"

He had a bravado I found really annoying, and I could see he thought I was having an anxiety attack or making the whole thing up.

"Just relax," he said. "It's all gonna be okay."

"Two thirty over a hundred," he called over the seat to the guy who was driving. "Pressure's off the charts."

"Thanks, buddy," I was thinking. If I had had enough energy, I would have asked him to keep my blood pressure to himself.

"Your friend on drugs?" He turned to Edna.

Since I had only met Edna a few months before, at a meditation retreat, she actually had nothing to go on.

"I don't think so," she said. "But I hardly know her."

By the time we got to the hospital, things were looking up. I was beginning to come to. I was able to breathe and started to get some color back, but because the paramedic who was riding in the back with me was so obnoxious, I didn't let on. I felt embarrassed, too, to have created such a scene when it now seemed like there was nothing wrong with me.

When the doors opened, Rachel, my favorite triage nurse, was there to greet me.

"You!" she said. "What's wrong now?"

"Same thing."

"Passing out?"

"Yep," I said. "I was out dancing. That's why I'm so dressed up."

"You look great!" she said. I had on my black cowboy boots, as I mentioned, and a black and white Mexican cowboy shirt, and, believe it or not, a wide-brimmed Mexican cowboy hat which, for some reason, the paramedics had failed to remove.

"Thanks," I said. "So do you."

"Okay. Let's get you started." She took my hat off and handed me a bag for my clothes.

21.

Dr. Jalili was a very nice man. Maybe he was thirty-five. His hair was short and neat, and he had the most beautiful olive skin that looked particularly striking against the white of his lab coat. Even his five-o'clock shadow was worth remarking.

"You just get married?" I asked. I noticed as he pulled the stethoscope from his neck that he was wearing a very shiny gold wedding band on the ring finger of his left hand.

"Yes, Ms. Glancy." he said. "Could you please lift your gown?"

He had an accent I recognized.

"Lebanon?" I said.

"Jordan," he answered.

"Deep breath," he instructed.

"I've been there," I said.

"Another."

For a moment I debated whether to tell him that I had lived in Israel for a year, had had sex with a Palestinian washing-machine repair man against the washing machine on spin, and then got pregnant by an Israeli guy ten years younger than me but lost the baby—my first of many —but decided, for the moment, it might not be a good idea to bring up Arab-Israeli affairs.

Dr. Jalili really was very cute and he smelled divine.

"I read the paramedic's report. It says you felt like you were going to pass out?"

I nodded.

"Your heart sounds strong. Your blood pressure's back to normal. Do you have any other symptoms?"

"I'm okay now," I said. "But I felt like I was losing it, like the world was slipping away."

Dr. Jalili crossed his arms over his chest. He was listening intensely; he looked genuinely concerned.

"I danced one dance, just one, granted it was a fast one, and then I felt like I was going to pass out."

"Does this happen to you often?"

"I was here last week. It just comes over me. I have no idea what's wrong."

"Hmmmm," he said. He sighed. His breath was sweet, and he was wearing some really lovely, warm, musky and citrusy cologne I recognized from the streets of Tel Aviv.

"Okay, Ms. Glancy, I think we will keep you a few hours to observe you, and then we will see what happens. Okay?"

"I don't think you're going to see anything," I said. "It comes over me suddenly, out of the blue, and not just from exertion, although that seems to bring it on. I feel very sick when I feel sick, like I'm going to die. When I feel like this, all I want to do is lie down on the floor and curl up into a ball. For some reason, I want to lie down on the floor."

"Hmmm," he said.

"I kind of get possessed, like an alien creature has invaded my body—and then it passes."

His eyes widened.

"But even when it passes, I still don't feel great. I feel really foggy and tired a lot of the time. I feel like I'm getting the flu, except it never comes. I just feel sick and near fainting and then sometimes it clears and I feel okay."

Dr. Jallili was nodding and sighing, tilting his head as he looked at me.

I had a flash, at that moment, a very vivid flash, of the time I was detained in Cairo by El Al security.

That day in Cairo I remember thinking the El Al security guy asking me questions was flirting with me.

"Do you always travel alone?" he asked, in a tone that at the time seemed almost playful. He had a little notebook, like a stenographer's pad, he held in front of his face. Seemed like everything I said he wrote down.

"Not when there's someone with me." I answered, winking at him.

"Hmmm," he said. "Okay, Miss Glancy. So where do you carry your passport?"

"That's a funny question!" I said, kind of laughing.

I was about to tell him I carried my passport under my shirt when, right at that moment, a dwarf wearing a three-piece suit and carrying two huge suitcases, one in each hand—I'm telling the truth here—passed through the very long security line without checking his bags or stopping to be questioned.

"What makes him so special?"

"Do you know that man?" the El Al security guy asked me pointedly.

"No, I don't know him! I just wondered why he doesn't have to stand on this line and be questioned like the rest of us!"

Things got serious very quickly. One moment, I was at the head of the line, flirting with Mr. Security. The next I was being led by two officials, a man and a woman, into a back room for further questioning. Two hours later, escorted by military police, I was allowed to board the plane. They even had to roll over a set of stairs just for me.

Now something about the way Dr. Jallili was looking at me made me think of that moment in Cairo. Was it that Dr. Jallili didn't believe me?

Nurse Rachel was standing next to him now.

"Right?" I said to Rachel. "Isn't this what happened the last time?"

She nodded.

"We'll keep her here a few hours," Dr. Jallili said to Rachel.

"I don't know what else to tell you, Miss Glancy," he said to me. "You've had a CT scan recently, and your heart sounds really strong."

The few hours I stayed in emergency were uneventful.

At about one in the morning, I fell asleep. When Rachel came to tell me her shift was over, I woke with a start. I had been dreaming, even though my neck was stiff from how I was propped up on the pillows she had given me.

There was a big reception for me—maybe I had won the Nobel Prize for Literature or had been voted Poet Laureate of the United States, something like that. I was calm and happy and very magnanimous, sipping on my champagne—when I realized we were inside an elephant! The walls were a rough brownish-gray, the texture of elephant skin. If the elephant sat up, all the tables would slide to one side, the glasses would break, it would be a disaster. But for the moment, it was all beautifully balanced—and auspicious. Being toasted inside an elephant was the highest honor anyone could ever hope to achieve.

Isn't that ironic? I was just thinking, inside the dream, *that there wasn't an elephant in the room, as the expression goes. The room was inside the elephant!* when I felt Rachel tap my shoulder.

"I'm off, darlin'," she said. "See you next time!"

"I hope not!"

"Me, too. No offense! It's always nice to see you. But really—I gotta run."

"Cool," I said. "Good for you."

When I sat up, I had wicked heartburn. Probably it was from all the almonds I had downed before I left the house in an effort to stave off — well, the inevitable.

"Oh, one more thing," I called to Rachel. "Sorry to bother you, but do you think you could get me a Maalox before you go?"

"Sure thing," she said. And once again put her hand on my shoulder. In a moment, she was back with one of those small plastic cups they use to administer meds.

"Thanks so much," I said. "I really appreciate it."

Excitedly, with the same cheeriness she always had in her step, Rachel winked at me and tootled off.

With Rachel gone, things got even more boring.

Edna had left much earlier, once Dr. Jalili arrived. The emergency room was really slow that night—no gunshot wounds, no heart attacks, no after-midnight DTs.

Eventually, I convinced Dr. Jalili that he might as well let me go home

"I may be back," I said. "But I don't think there's any more you can do for me now."

As usual, the hospital staff called me a cab, hugged me, and wished me well.

It always scares me at that hour—it was after two in the morning—to be alone in a cab in East Oakland. You just think the worst. I was always afraid the driver would steal my wallet, which I didn't even have with me, and dump me in the river.

He was a really nice guy, though, from Nigeria. Very smart. He told me he loved Alanis Morissette because she was "spiritual." That's what he said. He could tell from her lyrics.

Cara was asleep on the couch when I got home, and Marco looked like an angel, curled up in his crib.

I got into bed, set the alarm for six-thirty a.m., when I needed to get up and get Marco ready for preschool. It seemed like no matter what I did, I could only ever get four hours of sleep.

22.

The next day I see that my good friend Robert Marshall has commented on a comment about a post in which I am mentioned by the famous poet Eileen Myles.

"There's an homage to you at the end of Eileen's novel," Robert says. "You're a hero!"

At the end of her memoir-novel, *Inferno*, Eileen tells the story of the day we ran into each other in the East Village when we were cute, horny young poets, all revved up, as they say, with nowhere to go.

> It was gay pride weekend and I had marched down Fifth Avenue with Ann and Heather and we were looking for something to do so we wound up sitting in Mogador watching people go by. A writer named Gabrielle Glancy came by and sat down. She always had very interesting hair. Dark and pouffy like an empress. She showed us a flyer she had about a lesbian sex auction, celebrating gay pride. Would we like to go. We would. It took us a while to decide by eventually the four of us were walking across town.
>
> Like · Comment

These days I feel more like a ghost than a hero.

Many years ago, when I was a high school English teacher, I invited Eileen Myles to speak to my students.

"What is poetry?" someone in the class asked her.

She got up and stood in the threshold of the door.

Late afternoon light blazed behind and wrapped her in a swath of gold.

"Poetry," she said, "is a body in a doorway."

Photos by Lizy Mostowski

Saturday at 5:35pm · 🌐

Eileen Myles is one of my heroes.

She even ran for President in 1992.

I look closely at the pictures of Eileen Myles on Facebook.

In about 1985, I ran into Eileen Myles at Star Market on Avenue A in the East Village. She had a small square of adhesive tape over the bridge of her nose.

She looked excited to see me, I remember thinking, but also a little shy.

"How's life treating you?" she said, looking directly at me.

"Pretty good." I said, probably a little too quickly. I had just broken up with one lover or another. "And you?"

"Really good," she said, "Except my girlfriend threw a toaster at me and broke my nose."

Like me, Eileen Myles has not always been so lucky in love.

I bet she's not sick, I think to myself. *She looks alert, like she has a normal relationship to her own consciousness and unconsciousness, not random and scary like mine.*

Suddenly, I feel low, kind of queasy, deflated.

And then I think to myself: *How long have I had this crazy thing anyway?*

I remember taking a bike ride last August, during which I almost passed out. I thought it was the heat. That particular day, it was eighty-five in the shade at ten o'clock in the morning. It must have been over a hundred when I took my sparkling, new Cannondale Quick for a cruise.

So I guess it's been about nine months. Right before I fell into this state, my life was very active: I adopted Marco from Guatemala, built the cottage in my backyard—the one I rented to Cara and Gabriel—I turned fifty, threw a ball for myself, which

I hosted as a benefit for the Women's Earth Alliance, Caitlin's world-saving-organization-for-sustainability, and then had a brief and torrid affair with a woman, Renee, the last stop on my dating train. Like Caitlin, she wouldn't let me sleep over, though we had sex until four or five a.m. every night for the three months I saw her.

Sometimes when I left Renee's house, my body would twitch uncontrollably. I felt like I was losing my mind. I ate a lot of bananas those months. I attributed the twitching to a lack of potassium.

Sometimes I never slept at all.

Six thirty in the morning, I would send Cara home, shower, dress and feed Marco, and drop him at preschool before going to work.

I had the thought that the life I was living would be difficult to keep up. I noticed sores in my mouth—like canker sores—that would come and go, but I was never really tired. Perhaps I should have taken that as a sign. I didn't have any other symptoms to speak of.

It seemed sudden, the state I soon found myself in.

And now it has been nine months—that's a long time to be moving in and out of consciousness. And when I look at what I've done during that time—mostly, I've gone to doctors and facebooked. Really, that's just about all. Nothing much has really happened.

"I happened," Sudha says. "Aren't you going to say something about that?"

Marco looks at me strangely, like he's trying to see inside me. I often wonder what Sudha sees in me. Really wouldn't she want to be with someone more . . . I don't know . . . alive?

I look again at the pictures of Eileen Myles.

She's got a lot of friends. Four thousand two hundred and seventy-five. And how many books has she published?

For a moment, I think, *Why not just end it all right now?*

23.

After three visits to the ER, the same number of follow-up trips to see Dr. J, a visit to the ob-gyn, a CT scan and an EEG, an upper abdominal ultrasound, and about ten EKGs , the only definitive diagnosis I received after a full year was a vitamin D deficiency.

Dr. J was very proud of himself when the results of that particular blood test came in. He actually called me from his cell phone.

"Your numbers should be higher, Ms. Glancy. Normal is eighty-five, and you're at sixteen."

"Oh. Uh-huh," I said. "What does that mean?"

"It means you're severely deficient in vitamin D."

"What do we do about that? " I asked.

"Take vitamin D," he said.

"Could this deficiency be causing my symptoms?"

"I'm not sure," he said. "It can't be good."

"Why does someone have a vitamin D deficiency?" I asked.

"Do you drink?" he said.

"No."

'Take drugs?"

"Dr. J!"

"Eat meat?"

"Yes."

"Hmmm," he said. "Maybe you don't get enough sun."

So Dr. J called in a prescription for a hundred thousand units of vitamin D a day for a week.

"Let me know how it goes," he said. "It takes a while for the body to absorb. Check back with me in a month. We'll test you again and take it from there."

At first, as the days were getting longer, I would try to sit in the sun. Twenty minutes of natural vitamin D a day. Maybe this would help. If nothing else, it made me feel, kind of like Facebooking, that when I could do nothing else, at least I was doing *something*. But then this too became impossible. A few minutes in the sun and my state-of-conscious being would start to call it a day. I could feel it receding, like a distant train, slowly moving away. I was very pale that year.

24.

My fourth ER visit, when I began to come to, I realized I had a sharp pain under my ribs on the right side.

"How sharp is it?" the ER doc asked. He was wearing a black silky T-shirt and black, kind of dressy pants. His arms were brown and muscular, and he looked great under that shirt. He didn't look like an ER doc. No white labcoat. No stethoscope around his neck. He looked like he was going out to dinner after playing a round of golf.

"So, Ms. Glancy, how would you rate the pain on a scale from one to ten?"

"It ranges from a two to an eight and half," I told him. "But right now, it's a nine."

Dr. Alex Ng looked concerned.

"Hmmm," he said. "Show me again where the pain is."

I lifted my right breast and pointed underneath.

"Here," I said. "Underneath this breast."

"How would you describe the pain? Is it shooting, aching or throbbing?"

"It's aching and throbbing," I said. "And sometimes, it's shooting. Sometimes it's dull and sometimes it's sharp."

"Have you ever had this pain before?" Dr. Alex Ng asked. "Or is it a new pain?"

"Actually, " I began to remember, "when I was in London doing all my IVFs—I had four IVFs , that's a lot of IVFs, but it was cheaper in London—I had this pain. I remember it even shot around to my back. The nurse there said she thought it was from the hormones. I took a lot of hormones when I was trying to get pregnant . . ."

While I answered Dr. Ng's questions, I was trying to get his black eyes into focus, to gauge how close to the surface my waking mind was at that very moment, and to try to predict in which direction I was heading. Was I growing more alert or more dazed? Stalled in between, it was kind of hard to tell.

"Did you knock into something when you fainted?" Dr. Ng asked me.

"I didn't actually faint," I reminded him.

"When you got dizzy," he said. "Did you bang into anything?"

"Not to my knowledge," I answered.

"Tell me again, Ms. Glancy. Did you ever lose consciousness?"

"Not exactly," I said.

"What does that mean?"

"I mean, the feeling comes. I get spaced out and dizzy and my consciousness draws back; it recedes and I can't really think or talk. But I didn't actually go out. I mean not completely. I can still hear things but it's like I'm not really there."

"Hmmm," he said again. "Has this happened to you before?" he asked.

"Oh yeah," I said. "It happens a lot. I was here last week for the same thing. But sometimes it's really bad and I almost lose it and my heart starts to get weak."

"Hmmm," he said. "Do you still have the pain in your side?"
I nodded.

"How sharp is the pain now?" he asked.

The buzzing of the fluorescent lights was beginning to line up with my brain waves, and I was becoming less able to focus and talk.

"I've got to lie down," I said. "I guess the pain is an eight."

Dr. Ng prescribed morphine for the pain and suggested I stay a few hours so I could be observed.

The nurse who administered the morphine had long, dark brown hair that went down her back and blue blue eyes. She told me when I asked that she was from Australia.

"I've been there," I said. "Twice. How long you been here?"

"Ten years," she said. "Actually eleven in May. I should ask you how long *you've* been here." She was looking through my charts. "It looks like you live here!"

"Yea," I said. "I *feel* like I live here. I haven't seen you in the ER before. Are you new?"

The Australian nurse—her name was Roxanne—told me she had been on sick leave for the last three months.

"I'm not pregnant," she said. "I just look that way. My stomach is hard as a rock, and I feel weak all the time, not really tired, just like I'm gonna pass out."

For a moment, I felt like I was dreaming.

"That's so weird," I said. "That's exactly what I have!"

"It says here you have a pain in the upper right quadrant."

"I do, but that's not what I usually have. Usually I have what you just described."

"What *is* this?" I asked Roxanne.

"Damned if I know," she said. "But I can tell you, it's really debilitating. Sometimes I think there's something wrong with the water in America. I've travelled all over the world. I never felt like this before."

"You ready?" she said.

"Yep," I said. "Might as well."

Roxanne smiled, stuck the needle firmly into my arm, gave it a squeeze, and left the room saying, "It'll all be fine in a minute."

The morphine was divine.

At first I felt as if my entire body, from the neck down, came racing upward toward my head. In fact, it felt as if the hood of my sweatshirt had stuffed itself into the back of my neck.

"Nurse! Nurse!" I shouted, but by the time she got there, things were calming down.

However long the effect of the morphine lasted, I felt relieved of all my pain and worry—and completely cured of what had brought me into the emergency room in the first place.

Paradoxically, instead of floating, I felt, for the first time in many months, as if my vision was perfectly clear and my feet were planted firmly on the ground—I felt utterly alert.

The silver instruments on the rolling table seemed particularly shiny and vivid. I could almost see their sterility bursting out of their silver sheen.

The air was crisp and cool; I was full of sanity, clarity and health. I only wished I were somewhere more interesting where I could have really enjoyed it.

25.

Marc D'avegan Rubin shared PeaceLily's photo.

"There is not a particle of life which does not bear poetry within it"
— Gustave Flaubert

Like · Comment · Share · 4 minutes ago ·

Eve Hanninen likes this.

1 share

Write a comment...

On my good days, I feel like this.

26.

Desperate to find help, I finally texted Caitlin. Environmental lawyer by day, medicine woman by night, I figured she would be the one to call.

I had told almost no one what had been going on with me. It all just seemed too weird.

Sick for months, I wrote. And very sorry I had no compassion for you when you were. Am in weird state. Always almost fainting. Know anyone who might help?

Caitlin told me she had been seeing a Dr. Chew in Marin who was a "miracle worker," Caitlin said.

Worth a try, She texted. Good luck honey! And don't worry. You were nice.

27.

Dr. Melissa Chew, assistant director of the Solstice Center of Health in Sausalito had a sleek figure under her finely knitted dress. I had expected Dr. Chew to be Chinese and was surprised to see she looked a lot like the Marin moms whose kids I worked with every day. She wore a tight, knitted dress, high heels, and if I didn't know better, I would have pegged her as a banker's wife. Her dress was a purple color, just this side of egg-plant, cashmere perhaps—you could see the soft tendrils of its yarn reaching for the sun. It just about covered her ass—and she wore tights, a darker purple than the dress, and purple patent leather shoes, and her blond hair fell down the purple slope of her lovely back.

Dr. Chew's blue-grey eyes strained to see me through her contact lenses. It seemed that she was looking at the inside of her contact lenses rather than at me. Or at her computer, where she was doing research, even as we spoke, on the ins and outs of my mysterious condition.

"Tell me your symptoms again," she said.

I sighed. It seemed almost too much, but I knew I had to describe what I was feeling as accurately as I could in order to get help.

"Okay, " I said, taking a deep breath. "I have ongoing palpitations, maybe a thousand a day. Like just now, since I got here, I probably had twenty-five. My stomach feels like it's gonna explode. It gets rock hard like one of those exercise balls, and if I exert even a little, even walking to the end of the corridor"—I pointed down the hallway—"it starts to blow up like a balloon and seems to trigger some kind of reaction where I begin to faint. My consciousness pulls back"—I tried to demonstrate by putting my hands up and pulling them back behind my ears — "My field of vision starts to get smaller, my jaw locks up, and I can't really speak. I've already been to a neurologist and had two CT scans. My brain seems fine. The neurologist said I have neurocardiogenic presyncope—he gave me a handout to read—and it seems like I do have that—but then I also feel like why do I have palpitations and that speedy feeling and then everything seems to just come to a halt . . .?"

"Hmmmn . . . fainting," she said. And then I could swear she was googling every symptom I reported.

After a lot of hemming and hawing and on-the-spot research, Dr. Chew motioned me to the table.

The table had a sheepskin pad on it with white paper covering it, and it was a little higher than I expected. I actually had to use a chair to hoist myself up onto it.

Once I was on the table, Dr. Chew performed her miraculous acts of prognostication. That is, she asked me to extend my right arm into the air at an angle perpendicular to my body. Then she lay small, brown, medicine bottles on my chest "testing" my arm to see how much strength or resistance I had in relation to whatever she had put on top of me.

She mumbled things like "Magnesium, hmmmm" or "Yes, the zinc."

This took about two minutes. Dr. Chew was fast.

Then she asked me to put my shoes back on and said she would return with a diagnosis and recommendations in a moment.

I sat for a long time in her office.

I had seen a rainbow on my way there, right off the freeway, which I had stopped to photograph with my phone. The rainbow had come after a wild hailstorm—rare in California—hail the size of eyeballs, bouncing off the road.

Now the air was clear. The sun was peeking through the clouds. I looked out the window. I ran my hand against the side of her desk. There was a great view of downtown Sausalito from her office window and I found the curves of her blond wood desk very appealing.

Finally, Dr. Chew returned. She placed her firm knitted purple ass squarely on her chair, lowered her head and said something like:

"You have a magnesium deficiency, mercury poisoning, pre-diabetic glucose intolerance, a gluten allergy, and an iodine overload. In addition, you have low thyroid, overtaxed pituitaries, and ozone poisoning."

"Yes," she said. "I can see now why you're sick."

The supplements Dr. Chew prescribed cost me over three-hundred dollars.

"The important thing is that you cleanse," she said. "You're filled with environmental toxins that have caused imbalances and all kinds of other problems."

"Hmmmm," I said. "Anything else?"

"Yes, " she said. "Let's try an elimination diet. Let's take out sugar, dairy, gluten, soy, and citrus and see what happens."

"That's it?" I said. I was growing weaker now, the purple in her dress was blurring to a twilight haze, and I knew I needed to get something to eat quickly or I would begin to pass out.

"That's it," she said. "Come back in a month."

It was clear and bright, the streets still wet, when I left the Solstice Center of Health. Before I left Sausalito, I stopped at the market at the end of the street. I remember a high-end deli with prepared food where even the bananas seemed yellower and somehow more refined than the bananas you get anywhere else, as if they had been dipped in gold. I bought tri-tip in barbecue sauce, one royal banana, a bag of salted almonds, and a bottle of Smart Water to get me home. I noticed on the way out a small, covered stand that sold orchids. These also seemed more exquisite than any orchids I had ever seen. They were brilliant in color, also purple, and particularly vivid on this particular day. Was I high? I was beginning to go out. I thought for a moment I would buy an orchid for Sudha and drop it off on the porch in front of her apartment door, which was on my way home, but I was too weak to walk the twenty feet over to the stand. Once in the car, I downed my tri-tip and had a banana (it really was delicious) and conjured up just enough energy to get myself home.

28.

and then out of nowhere sun (as if to expose what of the hills—)
the white glare of x, the scathing splendor of y,
the wailing interminable _____?) ("To the Reader," Unified Field 61)

Like · Comment

I recognize this piece from a book by Jorie Graham. What ever happened to Jorie Graham anyway?

I seem to recall she was nominated for the Nobel Prize in Literature. Or am I making that up?

What ever happened to me?

I met Jorie Graham when I was twenty-eight at a writers workshop in Santa Fe where my parents built a house after they retired.

She told me to send the first poem I ever wrote to *The Paris Review* where it was published.

"I guess I'm a poet," I thought, and started writing poetry.

In my late twenties and early thirties, I had lovers and I wrote poetry. That's what I did.

Then one day, I decided to write a novel. I had been having a wild affair with a Russian woman ten years younger than me—my five-foot-nine-inch, brown/brown, unsociable, unpredictable, complicated, perverted, dis-balanced, artistic, narcissistic Russian/Jewish pessimist—who broke my heart.

While I was visiting her mother in St. Petersburg—she gave me old family photographs to bring home with me—Vera ran off with the pastry-chef-slash-painter she told me she had met the day before she met me.

The novel received a slew of stunning rejections.

"A page turner. Dazzling. But we can't tell, is it a memoir or is it a novel?"

"I love the writing. But where's the story?"

"I was intrigued, but I think you should change the ending. Vera should die, not disappear!"

After that, I kept writing, but I stopped sending out work. I guess you could say I went underground—but only for about twenty-five years.

Still, every time I think about it, I feel vaguely sick.

"Just do it!" Caitlin said. "You've manifested everything else in your life. What's stopping you from doing this?"

"I don't know what's wrong with me," I said.

And that was the truth.

29.

Wall Photos

Back to Album · Pakistan the Only choice's Photos · Pakistan the Only choice's Page

Like Comment

Pakistan the Only choice
The Silver Lining, The Spider Webs! An unexpected side-effect of the flooding in parts of Pakistan has been that millions of spiders climbed up into the trees to escape the rising flood waters. Because of the scale of the flooding and the fact that the water has taken so long to recede, many trees have become cocooned in spiders webs. People in this part of Sindh have never seen this phenome...non before but, they also report that there are now far fewer mosquitoes than they would expect, given the amount of stagnant, standing water that is around. It is thought that the mosquitoes are getting caught in the spiders web, thus, reducing the risk of malaria, which would be one blessing for the people of Sindh, facing so many other hardships after the floods...!!!

Like · Comment · Share · October 21, 2011

👍 52,930 people like this.

Sometimes I am moved by images and I don't know why. I stare at them a long time in a kind of curious daze. Then I take a screen shot of them and put them in my folder.

Sometimes I happen upon something so beautiful that it makes me want to cry. I don't cry, however. I can't remember the last time I shed a tear.

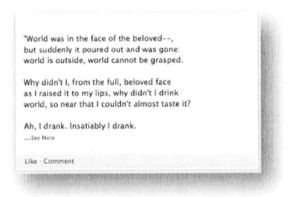

Oh Rilke . . . That's so beautiful, I think, drifting off into a state that feels much like this:

30.

Because Sudha's father had died of cancer when she was thirteen, she was deathly afraid of illness. Her own mother had lost both her parents in a car accident when she, too, was thirteen. For some reason—I guess to protect her—Sudha's mother didn't tell her that her father was sick until six months before he died. Instead, his illness was kept a secret. *Like a ghost in the house. Like a dark cloud,* she told me.

So when I ended up in the ER for the fifth time, we almost broke up.

Sudha said she was feeling "strange." She needed "space." She didn't know if she wanted to see me.

"What is it?" I said. "This seems to have happened suddenly."

"Have you fallen out of love with me?" I asked.

"It's not that."

"Are you afraid you're going to catch whatever I have?"

"Noooo . . ." she said

"Are you no longer interested?"

"I *am* interested."

"What is it? " I said. "It doesn't make any sense. So why do you want to break up?"

Finally, she came out with it.

"I'm afraid you're going to die." She began to sob.

I wished I could have said something to soothe her, but in fact, each time this crazy thing happened to me, I, too, thought this was it.

There was nothing I could say or do that would calm her.

Instead, I found myself underplaying my condition and limiting the time I saw her.

Lucky for me, Sudha had a more-than-full-time job and was often the one strapped for time.

When we did have a date, it was all I could do to stay with it.

Zane was "zaney," that's what I said about him. Beautiful, articulate, and off the wall—he was a handful. Marco, by nature calm, focused, and eager to co-operate, became wild and unruly whenever he was with Zane. And the two of them together—mayhem.

My patience was as thin as my consciousness. It was all I could do to breathe and stay alive.

The littlest thing made me want to explode.

One day I suggested we all go down with Marco. "We don't take naps," Sudha said. I could see she was appalled.

31.

And then, Christmas—all over Facebook.

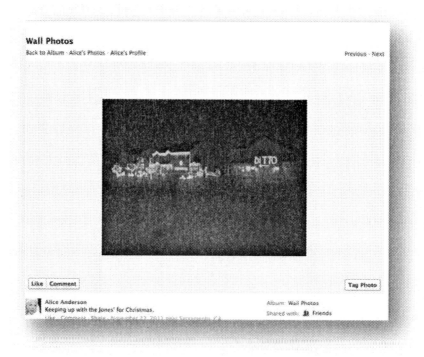

I couldn't think of anything scarier than Christmas. Suddenly, my symptoms started to get worse.

I knew it would require energy. I'd have to buy presents, go
to parties, don some holiday cheer.

It also meant Sudha would be on vacation, and probably she would want to spend more time with me. Under normal circumstances, this would have been what I wanted too.

And Marco—he would be off from school. How could I possibly spend days on end with him? Every few hours, I needed to eat or rest.

I was afraid I couldn't keep up appearances. Sudha would see the extent of my illness—and that would be it.

I'm not sure how I did it, but somehow, I pulled it off. I didn't even go to the ER once during the whole Christmas season even though Sudha, trying to make light of what scared her, would say: "It's been a month since we were in the ER, honey. Think you might like to drop in?"

The same time Sudha and I met—the week of my first visit to the ER—almost a year ago—she rediscovered skiing.

After eleven years in India, and more than that in the US, Sudha had not skied since she was fifteen. In fact, it had been twenty-three years when she asked me if it would be okay with me if she cut our holiday short and went with some friends to Tahoe right after Christmas to get back on the horse.

Her Swiss side—which she had all but forgotten when she left for India soon after her father died was suddenly—to my utter delight—reignited.

So Sudha and Zane set off for the slopes. Marco and I played Legos on the floor, took long, long naps and mostly stayed home. It was a low-key Christmas—which I thankfully survived.

32.

One night after work, I offered to help Sudha take down the Christmas tree we had all decorated a few weeks earlier.

It was the most perfect tree I had ever seen, the shape absolutely beautiful, as if each needle had been perfectly drawn.

I even posted pictures of the Christmas tree on Facebook.

Because we had not yet moved in together—although we spent Christmas at my house—we decided to put the tree up in Sudha's apartment.

Sudha sent me pictures on her phone.

"Beautiful," I said. "Magnificent. That's got to be the most perfect tree I've ever seen."

Sudha swore she watered it religiously, every other day, and got down under it to feel if its basin was dry.

"I even misted it once a week," she assured me.

But the ornaments were beginning to fall off.

"I don't understand it," she said. "It's wilting!"

"I never heard of a Christmas tree wilting, though sometimes they do dry up and lose their needles," I offered. "But they don't wilt!

Indeed, its needles were intact, but its branches had begun to droop.

One by one, the ornaments lost their hold and thudded to the carpet.

"Maybe we bought the tree too early," I offered.

"Maybe," she said, "the tree is sick."

Now here we were trying to take the thing down. How could we possibly get this seven-foot tree down three flights of stairs? I had hardly had enough energy to climb those stairs, let alone drag a sixty-pound monster of a wilting Christmas tree down them.

"I've got an idea," I said, trying not to lose face.

I remember my knees were wobbly, and everything was a blur.

"How 'bout we throw it over the balcony?"

"Yeah!" Zane squealed.

Sudha looked at me questioningly.

"I think it's a great idea! That way, we won't have to clean up all the mess!"

"No," Sudha said emphatically. "There's no way we are going to do that."

I could see the gears of her Swiss conditioning kicking in. Early on she had told me that in Switzerland it would be considered rude and improper to hang your laundry out on a Sunday.

"Only Italians do that," she said. "Swiss people would never do anything so vulgar!"

"Well," I said, "We could drag it down the hallway and try lowering it down the stairs?"

Sudha, Zane, and I stood in the middle of the living room looking at the tree. Piles of green needles outlined the felled fir like a halo. Even getting it off its stand had been difficult. It had taken two burly guys we accosted on their way to repair the roof to get it up the stairs in the first place.

Against Sudha's better judgment, we did throw the tree over the balcony. All three of us got behind it and pushed.

Then we ran down the stairs. I tied it to the back of my car and dragged it through the maze of hillside apartments to the

Christmas tree graveyard—a green dumpster that had been designated for this purpose—Sudha and Zane running behind the car.

33.

Winter was tough. There was nothing to look forward to and nothing to dread. It was just daily life near fainting. I muscled through work. There were times I had to excuse myself, go to the restroom, and lie down on the floor. I felt sick and sicker than sick. I saw Sudha as little as possible. I tried not to let Marco see me when it got really bad.

Still, I collected images.

34.

During this time, while Dr. J was on vacation, I staved off the ER with salt water, almonds, isometrics, and sheer acts of will.

The best thing I got from Dr. Chew at the Solstice Center of Health was a referral to the custom-compounding pharmacist, Peter Koshland.

It was Peter who had told me to drink salt water if I felt like I were going out. He also told me I could trick my adrenal glands into fight-or-flight by sticking my fingers down my throat to make myself gag.

"The gag response will keep you from fainting," he said. "It's kind of gross, but it works."

Crossing a major bridge like the Golden Gate in the condition I've been in poses a challenge. It would be a terrible moment to start passing out.

I used the gag reflex trick a lot.

Finally, when Dr. J returned, I was able to get a referral to a cardiologist.

35.

Dr. Ginny Peterson's office was special for Kaiser—she was head of the department. It had a pitched ceiling on the side where the examining table was, so the overhead light seemed very close. It was almost cozy in Dr. Peterson's office, in a sterile, hospital-examining room kind of way.

I was reading *The New Yorker* when Dr. Peterson came in.

"Ms. Glancy?" she said.

I nodded.

"You ready for me?"

"Yep," I said and put the magazine back in the rack that was hanging on the door.

"I was just reading your *New Yorker,*" I said. "I had a poem in there once upon a time."

Dr. Peterson looked impressed.

"Ginny Peterson," she said. She smiled and reached out to shake my hand.

Dr. Peterson put on her stethoscope and listened to my heart.

"It's beating," she joked. I watched her as she listened. She looked like she was from Wisconsin or Minnesota a few generations back. She had that pasty, honest, Midwest kind of look I associate with German immigrants who come from that area.

Her pale-blue eyes seemed sad, and her eyelids were red and inflamed. She looked very tired.

"I've been having palpitations of three different varieties for the last several months," I told her.

"I've got PVCs and two other kinds of arrhythmias," I said, looking up into her milky blue eyes.

She had confided in me that her brother, two years younger than she, had dropped dead a few weeks earlier of a heart attack. "And he had *low* cholesterol," she added.

"And he was a doctor, too," she said sadly.

"A cardiologist?" I asked, hoping against hope he was a dermatologist or something more benign.

She nodded. Again, sadly.

Dr. Peterson could hear no arrhythmias at the moments in which she pressed the cold silver disk to my chest. "But," she said, "sometimes they're shy."

A nurse came in and told Dr. Peterson they were closing the office. It was after 6 p.m.

"I can't find anything wrong with you," she said. "It could be hormones; it could be nerves. Your heart seems strong, though. I don't think you're at risk for a heart attack, and even though your cholesterol is high, like I told you, my brother had low cholesterol and look what happened to him."

I felt sorry for Dr. Peterson. She looked worn and, of course, she was grieving the loss of her brother, and probably wondering about her own health and her profession and how it all fit together—or didn't.

As she went over to her computer to write the whole thing up, I got off the table.

Suddenly, she looked up from her computer.

"Do you do yoga or meditation or anything 'spiritual' like that?" she said. "Anything metaphysical?"

"I know I should meditate," I said. "But to be honest, I rarely do."

"Huh," she said. "Hmmm."

"You know, there is something strange that happened to me recently, though, that for some reason I find myself wanting to tell you," I said.

She looked up, slowly, lovingly, I would have to say, from her keyboard.

"So, I was renting this office in Marin for the last year, while all this stuff has been happening. I had a weird feeling about the place, my office, I mean, like I was never alone there, like it was haunted."

She lowered her glasses. Now she really looked interested.

"So, last week, I ran into the woman who rents the office next door to mine. She's a woman in her sixties, a healer of some kind, a very lovely woman with red hair that's mostly gray now. She once helped me light the pilot on my heater . . . but that's beside the point . . . anyway, so last week I said: 'Westlynn, can I talk to you for a minute? You know, I've been in this office about a year and I've never felt good here. I've always felt a bit off. It feels 'funny' to me, kind of haunted.'"

"And what did she say?" Dr. Peterson piped up.

"She said, and you're not going to believe this, she told me a man named Paul, a very lovely man, she said, a therapist, had a heart attack in that very office just a year before."

Dr. Peterson was very calm in the way she was looking at me. She was nodding, almost as if she already knew what I was going to tell her.

"But this is the thing," I told Dr. Peterson. "I asked Westlynn what I should do to 'calm' the spirits, because I could feel they were unsettled in that office, and it was scaring me and making me feel weird.

"'Talk to Paul,' she said. 'He was such a lovely man. It was a real shock when he died. We were all very upset by it. The woman who cleans the office found him in there the next day. He had a heart attack.

'Tell him it's okay. You're in the office now. He doesn't need to be there.'

"So Westlynn left, my client came and went, and, once again, I was alone in the office, and it was time for me to pack up and go.

"'Paul,' I said. 'I don't really know how to approach this or what to say to you. I just want you to know I respect you. I mean your spirit, I mean.' I looked around at the tidy room with its dirty, white carpet, polyester curtains, and dull white-and-pale-purple paintings. 'I can feel you and I know you're here. If there's anything I can do . . .'

"But just at that moment . . ."

"I know what you're going to say." Dr. Peterson said.

"You do?" I asked.

Her eyes were calm and sad.

"It wasn't Paul," she said.

Now I really had the shivers. In fact, I thought I could feel something right then and there in that small space between the examining table, which still had the light shining on it, and the pitched ceiling, which was dark in the corners.

"The spirit wasn't Paul."

"That's right," I said. "It wasn't."

Dr. Peterson and I spoke in low voices even though, by now, we were the only ones left in the office.

"I got a message, some kind of sense, that the spirit that was in the office wasn't Paul's at all," I said. "And that this spirit wasn't a good spirit. It was evil in some way, malevolent—and, indeed, this was why Paul had a heart attack in the first place."

Dr. Peterson nodded.

"How did you know?" I said.

"I knew," she said.

I never went back to that office in Marin. In fact, a few weeks later, David, the landlord called to tell me my table was still there.

"Keep it," I said. "The place is haunted."

Because he was a friend of a friend, I thought I should warn him.

"Westlynn told me the story of Paul," I added.

"Uh huh," David said.

"I think there's a spirit in there, but I don't think it's Paul's."

"Oh, right," he said.

"I think whatever it is is why Paul had a heart attack in the first place. And I think you might want to think about getting out—I mean before it's too late."

"Okkkaaayy," he said. "Thanks."

My heart continued to beat arrhythmically, but, as far as Dr. Peterson was concerned, I was a picture of health.

"You're not going to die of a heart attack," she said and then added, kind of laughing. "But I'll order the tests anyway. We'll do an echocardiogram, a heart imaging test and a more in-depth EKG. And you'll have to have a stress test."

"A treadmill seems out of the question," I said. "I can't even walk from here to the door!"

Dr. Peterson assured me where there's a will, there's a way. "They can inject you with something that stresses your body and mimics the hormones released with intense exercise. It's very straightforward. How's Tuesday afternoon?" Dr. Peterson looked at me lazily over the top of her computer.

"I'm not sure I can withstand that much."

"You're stronger than you think," she said. "And the procedure is done in the hospital, so if anything happens, you're right there."

"I don't know," I said. "What do you think?"

"I think your heart is fine," she said, putting her hand on my shoulder. "As I said, I don't think you're going to die of a heart attack. Something else is going to kill you."

"That's reassuring!"

I laughed. She laughed. And then she turned back to her computer—to record her findings, I suppose—and I let myself out the door.

The five-minute walk to the parking lot to find my car seemed almost more than I could take. Unfortunately, I had left my salt water and my almonds in there. I prayed that I could make it down the elevator, across the street and up to level two of the garage without needing to call 911.

36.

In that perforated tunnel that lies on the road to unconsciousness, a dissipating scent, like a warm draftiness . . .

That's what I thought, something very much like that, but not in words, between sleeping and waking today after my afternoon nap. Vague, cloud-like images passed before my eyes . . .

I saw my head—not my head really, but my consciousness, as the stratosphere—like a satellite image of the earth with the ozone layer blown off. Suddenly I felt too exposed, like there was nothing protecting me. Everything could penetrate and get inside. . . . *That's it*, I thought. *That's why I'm sick. Too much can get inside . . .*

I thought to write it down, but I was just too out of it to move.

Sometimes I feel almost too tired to chase my own tail. But I know if I don't get out of this bed and chase it, I will perhaps float off into who-knows-where.

37.

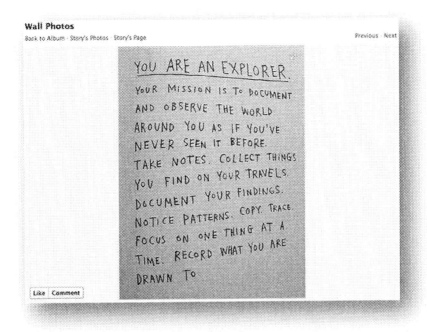

YOU ARE AN EXPLORER.
YOUR MISSION IS TO DOCUMENT
AND OBSERVE THE WORLD
AROUND YOU AS IF YOU'VE
NEVER SEEN IT BEFORE.
TAKE NOTES. COLLECT THINGS
YOU FIND ON YOUR TRAVELS.
DOCUMENT YOUR FINDINGS.
NOTICE PATTERNS. COPY. TRACE.
FOCUS ON ONE THING AT A
TIME. RECORD WHAT YOU ARE
DRAWN TO.

Like Comment

Yes, I think. *Without even knowing it, that's exactly what I've been doing.*

I realize it has been over a year that I have been collecting Facebook images and trying to describe what has happened.

When I tell my friend Ryan what I've been up to, he tags me in a post he had recently put up.

"You see," he says. "There are no accidents."

Never going to give you up never going to let you down never going to run around and desert you never going to make you cry never going to say Goodbye never going to tell a lie and hurt you.

You can't make this stuff up.

38.

Tuesday arrived.

I was brave and bold and got myself to the basement of Kaiser's main hospital, stopping to rest every few steps, drinking my salt water and trying to stay afloat. I had been to the basement of the hospital a few times before and it always seemed haunted and ominous to me. It smelled strange down there—a mixture of bleach, starch, and staleness—that's where they do the laundry. And, under this smell, another smell. The morgue.

Before I left the house, I took out the will I had written on yellow, legal paper.

I wish I could say it was not as bad as I thought it would be. In fact, it was worse.

The tech orderly strapped me to the table, gave me an IV through which the stress hormones would be injected and attached twelve wires to my chest and arms and legs. He was brusque and creepy. He had dark, stringy hair that came to points on his forehead. His open lab coat revealed long, dark chest hairs popping out of his shirt.

"I feel like Frankenstein," I said.

He didn't laugh or even crack a smile.

Then I tried to tell him how bad I thought it could get.

"Walking even a few feet sometimes causes me to pass out," I said. "What happens if that happens right now?"

"You'll already be lying down," he said. "Put your head back. You need to stay still."

"Could you at least describe to me what's going to happen?"

He was still fiddling with the wires. He seemed annoyed.

"It's very simple," he sighed. "Stress hormones are going to be released into your blood through the IV. This will make your heart race as if you're running as fast as you can."

"Oh God," I said. "I definitely can't take that!"

"We monitor your heart to see what effect this has on it. In a minute or two, the chemicals will wear off, and you'll start to feel normal again. That's how it works."

"No way," I said. "I'm not doing that. I think it could kill me."

"I doubt it," he said, looking down at his clipboard. "Okay, Ms. Glancy. Are you ready?"

"No," I said. "I've changed my mind."

"You want me to unhook you?"

Now he seemed really annoyed.

"Hey buddy, show some compassion!" I burst out. I would have said more but I was completely at his mercy.

I would have to take the test sooner or later, I reasoned. I might as well do it now.

I took a deep breath.

"Will anyone be here with me?" I said.

"I will," he answered. "Or you can press this red button for help." The tech orderly put a long, white wire in my hand that had a red button on the end of it.

"Okay, Ms. Glancy. We're going to begin the test."

Suddenly, the table I was on started tilting upward to an almost standing position.

In seconds, the chemicals were released into my blood. My neck started to expand and get tight as if it were going to explode; my stomach was in my throat; I felt as if skeins of liquid metal were pulling through my veins.

"You've got to stop this!" I said, looking around the room for the technician.

Where was he? Suddenly, I realized I was alone in the room.

The red button—I pressed it.

I pressed it again and again.

"William!" I screamed. I had looked at his name tag right before he left the room.

No one came.

Just then, the table started to descend. The chemicals too began to diffuse from the center of my body, through my arms and legs, and out.

And then William appeared.

He began to unhook the wires one by one, right arm, left arm, right side of chest, left, in the same methodical way he had hooked them in the first place.

"That was a nightmare," I said. "Why would you perform a test like this on anyone you suspect might be at risk of having a heart attack?"

William continued his menial task without looking up.

"I'm gonna report you," I said, finally. "You were nasty, and this is not going to go unreported. This kind of thing is not gonna happen behind close doors."

"Suit yourself," William said, crumpling the paper protector and throwing it in the garbage.

I got off the table and walked out the door.

In fact, I did report him.

At the desk where I had registered for the test, I told the receptionist.

"You should speak to the supervisor," she said.

"How do I do that?"

"I'll get him."

The receptionist left her post at the desk for a good few minutes. When she returned, there was a very trim, white-haired man with a red face and white lab coat following behind her.

"I heard you had a problem," he said.

"Your man William is evil. This test, which is already pretty intense, was traumatic. And really what you need is someone civil, someone who actually cares."

"Yes," he said. "I understand. We've had this problem with him before. You should fill out a report. The forms are over there."

I was trembling, from the chemicals and the stress, but I filled out a report.

It was all I could do to get home.

I hummed "I Will Survive" all the way to keep from hyperventilating, downed my salt water, and munched on almonds.

39.

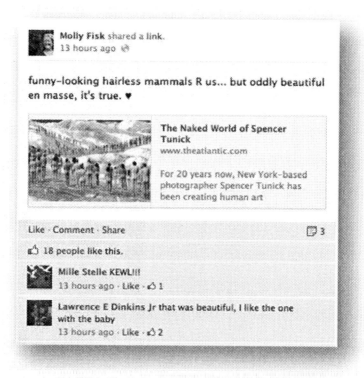

Molly Fisk shared a link.
13 hours ago

funny-looking hairless mammals R us... but oddly beautiful en masse, it's true. ♥

The Naked World of Spencer Tunick
www.theatlantic.com

For 20 years now, New York-based photographer Spencer Tunick has been creating human art

Like · Comment · Share   3

18 people like this.

Mille Stelle KEWL!!!
13 hours ago · Like · 1

Lawrence E Dinkins Jr that was beautiful, I like the one with the baby
13 hours ago · Like · 2

I click on the site.

For a moment, I am mesmerized.

The images seem innocuous enough. Other people were moved and impressed—I can see from their comments. But for some reason, it starts to scare me, creep me out.

Are they waving to the naked statue?

Look at all those bodies curled like folds of the brain.

Later, in half sleep, I see it clearly. And it scares me, irrationally. I feel like I'm going crazy.

We're larva! I think.

I don't even know how to describe the feeling seeing these pictures give me. It's like being in a dark alley that smells of urine during a Christmas party a hundred years before you were born.

Finally, that night, on the road to sleep, I have a sense of it.

We're larva! We're nothing but hairless worms. And we never grow up. We're larva all our lives.

40.

Dr. J stood tall and looked cool in his pale, sage-green shirt that hung loosely from his shoulders.

"Hi, Ms. Glancy," he said. He bent over and shook my hand. "How are you feeling?"

I had left Marco with my eighty-two-year-old parents, who were staying less than a mile from my house. My mother had dragged my dad across the country to find a doctor who would do laser surgery on her back. Out of her mind with the pain, she was heavily sedated.

"Call us from the hospital," she said. "Tell 'em they gotta take you. Tell 'em there's no more fooling around!"

Before I left the house, I once again grabbed my will, packed my daypack with extra clothes, my computer, and my cell phone charger.

I felt too sick to drive. I was weak and dizzy, so I called Deluxe Cab of Oakland to come pick me up. A Sikh driver wearing a midnight-blue turban whisked me off to the hospital.

"Ms. Glancy?" Dr. J said again.

I stared at Dr. J through the jittery haze that was my vision as if I were inside a warbled glass bottle or as if he were speaking to me in another language.

"Are you feeling better?" he asked, perfectly earnest.

"I'm dying," I said.

He let out a nervous laugh.

"Before I left the house, I wrote a will. I'm very, very sick, Dr. J. I'm sicker than I've ever been in my life."

He looked concerned.

"Tell me your symptoms again, Ms. Glancy."

"I've told you a million times!" I said, rallying enough to speak. "This is the fourth time I've been here this month. My symptoms are exactly the same. Suddenly, out of nowhere, my stomach becomes hard as a rock, and I get lightheaded like I'm about to faint. My consciousness draws back and I can't talk . . . I feel like I'm gonna die . . . I'm not in this state all the time, but often enough. The rest of the time I feel like I'm just about to get the flu. My body aches; I'm spaced out and racey all at the same time; I just feel really really sick!"

"Do you ever have tingling in your hands when this happens?"

"Sometimes. I have palpitations, not just during an episode, but all through the day. I have like maybe a thousand of them a day."

"Hmmm, " Dr. J said.

"And I get hot and cold. My hands get hot like they're burning up, like two hundred degrees, and then I start shaking, trembling up and down my body."

"Hmmmm," Dr. J said again.

"Ms. Glancy, I don't want to upset you, but your symptoms sound very much like anxiety. Maybe you're having panic attacks.

"Panic attacks?"

"Are you familiar with what a panic attack is?"

"Familiar with them?" I said. "I'm the panic attack queen! I know exactly what a panic attack feels like, and these are not panic attacks, Dr. J. Feeling like you're going to pass out while driving over the Golden Gate Bridge makes me nervous, granted, but I'm not passing out because I have anxiety. I have anxiety because I'm passing out!"

Now I was really fuming.

"Of course you would say that it was all in my head," I added. "That's what women are like, right? We're hysterical!! What, did we just turn back the clock two hundred years? I'm sick, Dr. J. I'm not crazy!"

"Okay, Ms. Glancy, okay."

He sat down at his computer. He took a deep breath and started over.

"I see you were in the ER again last night."

"Uh-huhhhh," I said, sarcastically.

My whole body was trembling and I felt like I wanted to cry.

"It says here you had a CT scan, an EKG, and were given morphine? What was the morphine for?"

"I had a sharp pain under my ribs on the right side."

"Everything looks normal," Dr. J said. "What did the ER doc say when they checked you out?"

"He said I had the heart of a thirty-year-old, a very clean brain—whatever that means—and that the pain in my side was probably a pulled muscle from excessive masturbation. I shook his hand; I shook the hands of all the nurses (most of them know me), and then I took a taxi back home."

"And what brings you here today? Do you still have the pain in your side?"

"What brings me here today is that I'm dying! Something is eating me up from the inside out. I feel completely possessed! And whatever it is is eating my stomach, my food, my heart, *and* my brain. It's taken me over. I know it sounds crazy, but, honestly, this is what it feels like. I'm sick and I'm dying and I'm not leaving here until you admit me to the hospital!"

"Ms. Glancy," Dr. J said.

"I'm deadly serious, Dr. J. I want to be admitted!"

Dr. J looked sad and a little scared.

"Ms. Glancy . . ."

"Dr. J."

"I can't admit you."

"Yes, you can."

"It's not that simple."

"I'm not leaving until you do. I'm sick and I'm dying. My parents are here from Florida. I got care for Marco, at least for a few days. And here's my will!"

At this point, I was shouting.

"Suit yourself, "I said. "But if you won't admit me to the hospital, I'll die right here!"

For a moment, I thought I saw a hint of anger on Dr. J's otherwise kind and implacable face. And then there was a knock on the door.

"Yes," Dr. J said.

The Indian nurse who had registered me poked her head in.

"Is everything all right?" she said.

"Yes," Dr. J said. "Everything's fine.

The nurse pulled her head back out and shut the door.

I was relieved Dr. J didn't continue our absurd conversation in the presence of the nurse, who might have supported the idea that I be admitted—to the psych ward.

"Please, Ms. Glancy," Dr. J continued. " Understand. I can call an orderly who can take you to emergency, where they can admit you if they see fit, but I myself can't admit you to the hospital."

"That's fucked!"

Dr. J looked startled. It can't have been the first time he heard the word, but somehow, it seemed, I had gone too far.

I loved him, but I was furious.

And so, against my better judgment, I continued.

"It's fucked that you have to send me to emergency just to admit me to the hospital. In fact, that's crazy. The whole health care system is crazy—the whole system is fucked!"

My words echoed in the air.

It was terrible what was happening. And it was sad. There was no turning back now. It would mean I would have to leave Dr. J.

Dr. J looked down at his computer and resumed his typing.

Since computers were installed in the examining rooms, by the way, I have noticed that doctors spend more time on their computers than they do with their patients.

In fact, ridiculous as it was, it seemed to me that Dr. J, all adorable seven feet of him, was hiding behind his screen.

I sighed.

"Okay," I said.

Dr. J looked up.

"Call an orderly."

This was my sixth emergency room visit in just as many months. And my second visit in less than twenty-four hours.

Dr. J ordered a wheelchair from transportation, and a very nice orderly helped me into it and carted me off to the ER.

My favorite nurse, Rachel, all cute, blond five feet of her, was still on duty.

"You're back!" she exclaimed. "Now what happened?"

"Same old story, " I said. "They won't admit me to the hospital unless you tell them I'm sick."

"Acchhh," she said. "That's too bad. I'm so sorry. Okay, get undressed," she handed me a gown and a bag for my clothes. "We'll do our best to find something wrong with you!"

That's the last time I saw my beautiful Dr. J . Bless his heart. I just wonder why when I said "Something's eating my food," he didn't take that as a sign.

41.

Dear Miss Kidd,

Ursula K. Le Guin writes extremely well, but I'm sorry
to have to say that on the basis of that one highly
distinguishing quality alone I cannot make you an offer
for the novel. The book is so endlessly complicated by
details of reference and information, the interim
legends become so much of a nuisance despite their
relevance, that the very action of the story seems to
be to become hopelessly bogged down and the book,
eventually, unreadable. The whole is so dry and
airless, so lacking in pace, that whatever drama and
excitement the novel might have had is entirely
dissipated by what does seem, a great deal of the time,
to be extraneous material. My thanks nonetheless for
having thought of us. The manuscript of The Left Hand
of Darkness is returned herewith. Yours sincerely,

The Editor

21 June, 1968

FROM ARTHUR C. FIFIELD, PUBLISHER,
13, CLIFFORD'S INN, LONDON, E.C.
TELEPHONE 14430 CENTRAL.

April 19 1912.

Dear Madam,

I am only one, only one, only one.
Only one being, one at the same time.
Not two, not three, only one. Only one
life to live, only sixty minutes in one
hour. Only one pair of eyes. Only one
brain. Only one being. Being only one,
having only one pair of eyes, having
only one time, having only one life, I
cannot read your M.S. three or four
times. Not even one time. Only one look,
only one look is enough. Hardly one
copy would sell here. Hardly one. Hardly
one.

Many thanks. I am returning the
M.S. by registered post. Only one M.S.
by one post.

Sincerely yours,

Miss Gertrude Stein,
27 Rue de Fleurus,
Paris,
France.

Darling,

This office has taken a long time to say no to Nabokov's *Lolita* which you and I both know was impossible at least for us. Do you want the books back? I don't imagine so in which case we will keep it for our blank department. But let me know. I wonder if any publisher will buy it.

Will you please tell Renée that I had her charming letter. I have no news except that the Coco is holding his own. As soon as I know more, I will write. But it was enchanting of her to send me a line, and I am very grateful. We have all been upset about this affair.

Bless. And all the best.

Thank you for posting this, anonymous friend number 1,257. You made my day.

42.

My tender underbelly, surrounded by the hazy membrane of semi-consciousness that intermittently keeps me at a distance from the world.

Fiona Capuano shared Wild for Wildlife and Nature's photo.

Baby Stingray ♥ (they are called pups)

Stingrays are usually very docile and curious, their usual reaction being to flee any disturbance but, they will sometim...

Like · Comment · Share · 3 minutes ago · 🔗

Felix Green Looks like a lizard trapped inside a membrane...
a few seconds ago · Like

43.

While all this was going on, I was falling in love—albeit in a way I didn't recognize.

Is this love or isn't it?

Am I awake or am I asleep?

How are you supposed to know anything when your *being* state is coming and going like clouds in the sky?

Whatever the case, for the better part of our first year, I experienced Sudha as slightly *over there*.

Whatever the cause, there were moments I felt a sea of I-don't-know-what between us, and a hint of sadness at feeling this way.

And yet at other moments, the fog lifted, and I had a feeling I have rarely felt that is beautiful—and clear—and felt like it might be love.

"There is this pool," Sudha told me. "You must come see it."

After she left the "mold house," which was the first place Sudha ever lived by herself, she moved into one of these hillside apartments in Larkspur overlooking the valley that reminds her of her childhood home in Switzerland, the one overlooking Lake Zurich, the one her father died in, the one her mother lives in still.

There's always a wind in the pines up there; the air is thinner; the sun seems to shine a little more brightly.

Sudha had been trying to get me to go to this secret pool since we met. Indeed it sounded magical, but I wasn't sure I could make it.

"How do you get there?" I asked, nervously.

"I found this trail," she said. "It winds up the mountain and down behind the apartment complex. There's never anyone there, and it's not heated."

We had taken the kids a number of times to the pool at her apartment complex—the regular one, not the secret one—and it was sickeningly warm with a smell we later identified as more than vaguely like vomit.

"The water's cool—it's completely empty there," she told me, "and it's crystal clear!"

"Yes," I said. "Definitely," I said. "As soon as we have the time."

Finally, unable to resist her entreaties any longer, I agreed to go.

Breathlessly, I climbed the eleven stairs to her door. Usually when I came to visit, I tried to tiptoe so she wouldn't hear me, because I needed a moment to recover before I knocked. In fact, I usually rested two or three times on the way up.

This particular day, Sudha was waiting for me at the top.

She looked ravishing. Her hair was swept to one side, her green eyes were clear and sparkling, and she had on my favorite low-cut shirt.

"Wow," I said. "Wow-ee."

I was too embarrassed to do what I usually did, so I took all eleven stairs without stopping.

When I got to the top, winded and starting to feel strange, she kissed me like never before, pulled me through the doorway, and took me right there in the foyer, standing up.

I was amazed and disoriented—and losing consciousness all at once.

I was swept up into the moment and—much as I tried to hold on—little by little, I was losing ground.

Finally, in the heat of passion, my body froze. Just as it always happened, my stomach blew up, my jaw locked, and my mind said *toodle-oo*.

Through a blank curtain of numbness, I managed to say: "Uh-oh."

"What, honey?" she said. "What is it?

"Salt?" I said.

Sudha ran into the kitchen to get it. I kept a stash of Himalayan sea salt wherever I might need it.

I could hear the spoon clinking against the glass. As early as it was in our relationship, she knew exactly what to do.

I was hoping the salt water would do the trick, as the other methods I had learned to keep from passing out were even less attractive than the act of passing out itself. The less egregious of the two was an isometric exercise in which you press the back of one forearm again the inside of the other in order to get the blood back to your head. And the second— the least appealing, but more effective—was to make myself gag.

Thankfully, the salt water and isometrics staved off a faint.

"I'm so sorry," I said. "Passing out is not very romantic."

"Don't worry," she said, but I could see she was worried.

"I guess you don't want to go to the pool today," she said. I could hear her disappointment.

"I'm sure I'll come to. Just takes me a minute."

Thirty almonds, two glasses of salt water with Himalayan sea salt, and a Greek yogurt later, I wanted to give it a try.

"You sure?" she asked. "We *could* do this another day."

"I'm OK," I said. "As long as we take it slow."

We stopped a hundred times on our way up the mountain and down. Sudha held my bag of almonds and my water bottle, because it was too much for me to carry them.

"Please," she said. "Let's turn back."

"We've already gone at least halfway," I answered. "At this point, it's the same distance back as forward. Let's press on."

And so we did—through redwood trees on dusty half-worn trails, the dry smell of sage and pine in the air, in what seemed like an endless journey to paradise.

There it was.

A beautiful, clear, rectangular pool, turquoise blue, over-looked by nothing, surrounded by a wood fence, and perched on a hillside of swaying trees.

It was every bit as beautiful as Sudha had described, and there was no one else there.

Sudha took off her clothes. In an instant, she was in the water.

When she came up, she was beaming. Her green eyes glistened.

"Come," she said.

"You swim. It's gonna take me a minute to recover."

I watched her naked breaststroke, her body lithe in the water, her head cutting through it like a prayer.

I looked around at the trees in the wind, the blue sky behind them, felt the air crisp and clear, the sun on my face.

I could fall for this girl, I thought. I'm really in trouble now. She could be my one.

44.

One day I realized it wasn't all in my head, it was in my stomach.

For one, I had learned to stave off the strange state long enough to somehow be able to observe and isolate the sensations.

Completely out of almonds, one morning, when I thought I was going to faint, I turned to Marco's Lowfat Wallaby Lime Yogurt.

Within minutes, my entire body went into a sort of convulsion. I still have no idea why, but what I saw was that the initial catalyst for my cascade of symptoms was decidedly—abdominal.

It was because I was painfully nauseated, dizzy, and sick with some sort of exhaustion connected with my stomach, that I wanted to lie down on the floor and die.

Later that week, I drove through the valley of ashes that is Richmond, California, through deserted streets and boarded-up businesses to Kaiser Richmond, in order to be seen by the top gastroenterology dog, Dr. Janet Joan Miller.

I sat in the waiting room, waiting.

I sat and waited a very long time.

I saw many people going in the in door and coming out the out door while I sipped on my Himalayan sea salt water disguised in a Smart Water bottle and ate my nuts.

Finally, I asked the receptionist what was going on.

"I'll check," she said and disappeared down the corridor.

In a moment, she was back.

"Sorry, Miss Glancy. She's here. There must have been a misunderstanding," she said. "I'm not sure what's happened, but come through this door; I can get you into a room."

Once in the examining room, I sat and waited, just I had done in the waiting room.

Dr. Janet Joan Miller was an hour and forty-seven minutes late for our appointment, which was scheduled for nine o'clock in the morning.

Actually, she had waltzed into her office at nine fifteen—I recognized her from her website photo—but evidently, it took her an hour and thirty-two minutes to fix her hair.

During this time, I read the brochures on diabetes, ulcer, colonoscopy, GERD, and stomach cancer; I looked at the diagram of the duodenum; I had checked my email before setting out from the examining room. I only had a few hours to spare before I needed to eat. At this stage of my illness, my salt water and nuts only took me so far.

Dr. Janet Joan Miller's office was right down the hall from the examining room I was in.

I saw her name on the door and decided to poke my head in.

There she was at her computer, fixated.

I couldn't believe it.

"Dr. Miller?" I said.

"Just a minute," she said, without even turning around.

"I've been waiting over an hour for you! I'm in room four. Do you think you can come in and see me now?"

"I said, 'Just a minute,'" she said.

I couldn't believe my ears.

"Dr. Miller!" I said, raising my voice.

At this Dr. Janet Joan Miller began to dislodge herself from her computer and rolled back her chair—just enough so I could see what she had been doing.

Dr. Janet Joan Miller was on Facebook.

Dr. Janet Joan Miller wore a tight dress that had a silver sheen and little red flats and spoke to me in a strangely quiet voice. She kept cocking her head and looking at me like a Tibetan terrier startled by unusual sounds. Her head tilted sideways, she would suddenly focus on one area of my body or another, like my right shoulder or my hair, dreamily, and for a long time, as if no one were watching her. But of course, I was watching her.

Finally she said, "OK, so tell me, what is happening?"

"I feel like something's eating me from the inside. Eating my stomach and eating my food. And I feel like my stomach's exhausted."

She let out this wild laugh, then a kind of sarcastic laugh, and said, "Exhausted? Now what's that supposed to mean?"

"It's the only way I can explain it. I feel like my stomach is tired, like the walls of my stomach have been working overtime, and they want to take a break, but they just have to keep going."

She began looking at me in that strange way again, focusing on me with her head bent sideways as if she were in a kind of trance. Had she seen something in my chart?

"Dr. Miller?" I said.

Then she put her hands together and bent over a bit, making her dress tighten across her thighs. "Now really, Ms. Glancy," she said imploringly, "What could possibly go wrong in the short distance between your mouth and your anus?"

I couldn't believe my ears.

"What could possibly go wrong?" I said. "Hell if I know. Isn't that why you went into gastroenterology? I only know something *did go* wrong. I just don't know what it is. That's why I came to you!"

Dr. Janet Joan Miller recommended I have an endoscopy and a colonoscopy. Whatever was going on could not be seen from the outside. Clearly, we needed an inside view.

45.

When I got home from the valley of ashes, Prahbhavita and Eyal, friends of Sudha's from India, were visiting from their commune. She had asked me if they could sleep in my guest room, just for a night.

"You better warn them," I had said. "Otherwise, if it happens, they'll wonder what the hell is going on."

So there they were, with Sudha, in my backyard. I was exhausted and losing hope I'd ever find out what was wrong with me.

They had come to California to trim weed so they could make enough money to return to their commune for another six months.

"Hi, all," I said, hoping to slip past them into my office.

"Have you heard about chemtrails, Gab?" Sudha asked. Clearly, she was stoned.

I hadn't.

"Apparently, the government drops chemicals over urban areas to sedate people so they can control them."

"Huh," I said. "That wouldn't surprise me. I know I feel pretty weird."

"We heard you're . . . sick," Prabhavita said, kind of shyly.

128

I felt pretty wobbly and just wanted to be alone.

"I don't know if I'd go that far, " I said. "It's just for some reason, I'm prone to passing out."

Prabhavita looked concerned.

"Prabhavita showed me pictures, Gab, from Facebook," Sudha piped up. "We wondered if you might be suffering from environmental poisons dropped out of planes by the government."

"Thanks, honey, but I don't think so. That would be an easy answer, for sure. But I think it's deeper than that."

Then I turned to Prabhavita and Eyal to excuse myself.

Although I knew they were high as kites and I couldn't quite take them seriously, I had a moment of hope—and terror.

Maybe that was what was wrong with me: I'd been sprayed with chemicals that had completely wreaked havoc on my body. Or if it wasn't chemicals, maybe it was bacteria . . .

Certainly I felt full of toxins. And as if my body, the healthcare system—and the whole fucking world of politics and medicine—had betrayed me.

Who was to say this wasn't the result of something the government drummed up and dropped from the sky?

"Sorry to be such a party pooper, " I said. "But I think I'd better lie down. I'm gonna have to let you finish this conversation without me."

46.

Once inside my office, I facebook chemtrails. Maybe there is something to it.

Chemtrails Awareness
April 19, 2011

"A nation can survive its fools... but it cannot survive treason from within. For the traitor appears not a traitor; he speaks in accents familiar to his victims, and he wears their face and their arguments, he appeals to the baseness that lies deep in the hearts of all men.

Like · Comment · Share   👍 72 💬 29 ⬜ 2

Topwater Tony ▸ Chemtrails Awareness
April 6

il clouds 2012

Like · Comment · Share   👍 6 💬 3

That white stuff you see in the sky—I don't know about you, but to me it looks very much like clouds—cirrus clouds to be exact.

And yet, ridiculous as it seemed, Prabahvita and Eyal's suggestion started to seem plausible. In any case, it got me thinking. What if, because the ozone layer had burned off, chemicals that could make us sick could now penetrate the atmosphere? What if I was somehow more susceptible than others? My skin thinner?

Images from *The Andromeda Strain, Invasion of the Body Snatchers* . . . it exhausted me just to think about it.

What if? What if? What if? . . . as I drifted off to sleep.

47.

Dr. Janet Joan Miller's assistant, a very small woman who told me twice she was from the Philippines, gave me the details of the endoscopy and colonoscopy before I left Dr. Janet Joan Miller's office.

It all seemed straightforward enough. First a twenty-four-hour fast during which you drink a liquid that makes you go.

"So they can get a good picture," she said.

Then an IV that fills you with twilight anesthesia, a tube down your throat, and a probe up your ass.

I made the mistake of having Sudha drive me. We hadn't been dating that long. She was awkward and anxious the whole time.

The nurses in outpatient surgery were unable to get a vein.

"Hard stick," they kept saying as they passed the paraphernalia from one to the other.

Try as they might, they just could not get the IV in. Finally, they called an oncology nurse.

"She's in chemo," they reassured me. "If she can't do it, no one else can."

Monique, the oncology nurse, was indeed a wizard. She had magenta nails three inches long.

"What did I ever do to you?" I said, as she slapped the back of my hand to bring the veins to the surface. "I'm not squeamish at all. It's just my veins that are shy."

Within seconds, she got it.

"You're an angel from heaven."

"Flattery will get you everywhere," she said. And then to the orderly, "Okay, she's yours."

There was Dr. Janet Joan Miller wearing scrubs and a mask over her face.

"Okay," she said. "Let's get started."

In moments, the ceiling dissolved into blue powder.

Next thing I knew, I was violently gagging. I felt as though she were beating a drum inside me and I just wanted to get it out.

"Fentanel," I heard Dr. Janet Joan Miller say.

The probe in my mouth knocked against the deepest part of my esophagus until, I suppose, it was lowered into my stomach.

That's the last thing I remember before waking up in recovery.

"You have a duodenal ulcer the size of a quarter. Take Omeprazole for a month, and it'll be gone. You don't have Barrett's esophagus. Not even close. Your colon looked great, completely clean. I'm sorry to say I couldn't find anything else wrong with you."

I guess she answered her own question: "What *could* possibly go wrong in the short distance between my mouth and my anus?"

It was not until I got home and looked in the mirror while brushing my teeth that I realized, with horror, that the whites of both my eyes were completely red. I guess the blood vessels had broken as a result of all the gagging.

I also had a black eye.

"You look battered," Sudha said. "She really got you."

Clearly, it would have been prudent to have waited to register my complaint against Dr. Janet Joan Miller to the Board of Grievances at Kaiser Hospital until after the procedure had been completed.

48.

The night after the endoscopy and colonoscopy, Sudha slept in the living room because I kept jolting awake. It seemed as soon as I fell asleep my body began reliving the endoscopy that my mind only half remembered.

After the third or fourth time, I decided it was safer to stay awake.

It was four a.m. by this point, and, of course, the only thing I felt like doing was what I always felt like doing when there was nothing else I could do.

I scan my newsfeed for something to catch my attention. For a long time, there is nothing, nothing, nothing.

And then I see something quite miraculous—a photo of a fly someone created out of dust bunnies. A perfectly formed fly or maybe a moth—dust-colored, beigey, yellowy, gray—antennas and all.

I look at it a long time before moving on.

Then I see a cool photo of Eileen Myles—with a piece of one of her poems on her T-shirt.

Eileen Myles was tagged in Tamara MC's photo.

During our poetry workshop at SLS in Lithuania.

Indeed, I think, *this body already feels like a corpse.*

Then an image of those same naked people that creeped me out in the first place—this time in the shape of a brain.

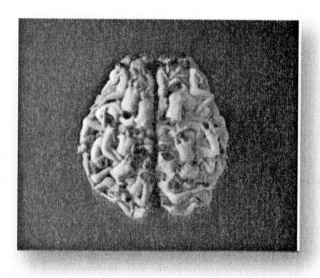

And a poem by some young new poet named Ish Klein.

We Will Free Each Other

Yes, yes larval. Larvalous was eye—the stars,
they were wondering, "When is X coming out?
Considering the material, X will be something!"

A glamorous anus was the mark of the sentiment.
And then, and then came the actor.
The dork who wanted form. And he figured
where the seeing-me-capacity was and he watched me be.

Uncanny how everything I am seeing seems to be telling my story back to me. Maybe the aftereffects of the anesthesia?

Just as I am about to throw in the towel and try to go back to sleep, I have this desire to see again that image of the fly or moth or whatever it was made out of dust and to put it in my file. But when I look for it, it's gone! Where could it be? Could someone have posted it and deleted it, just like that? I can't remember who had put it up in the first place. Was it a dream?

I try for a long time to find it.

49.

During the entire time I was sick, I only missed one day of work. It was the day after the endoscopy. I was smart enough to cancel all my appointments ahead of time. Looking like I had been beaten up wouldn't have done a whole lot for my reputation.

As it turned out, Marco's babysitter called in sick that day, too, and so Marco and I spent the day together.

"Baby Mommo needs to take a nap," I said to him after breakfast. "What does Mommy Marco want to do?"

After lunch, while Marco sat on the living room floor playing with his blocks and tiles, in a haze of half-sleep and afternoon fog, I logged on to Facebook in hopes once again of finding the image I had lost.

"What are you doing, Mommo?"

"I'm looking at pictures."

"Can I see?"

So Marco sat on my lap and looked at Facebook with me.

"There we are, Mommo!" Marco exclaimed, very excited. He was pointing to the tiny image of us—my profile picture—on the screen.

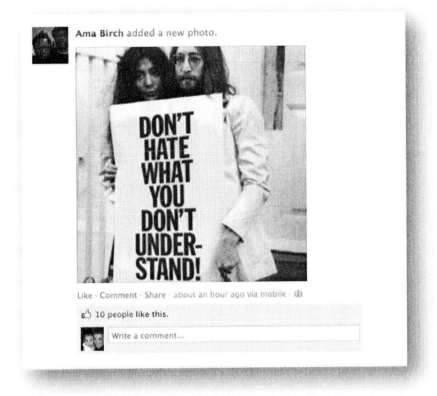

Indeed, there we were—Marco, just off the boat, and me, cute and healthy, before all this happened.

"Who are those people, Mommo?" Marco asked.

"That's John Lennon and Yoko Ono," I told him.

"Mommo," he said. "There we are again!"

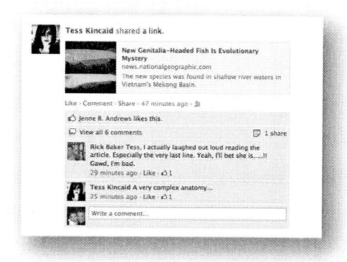

"What kind of fish are those?"

I clicked on the article to show Marco some more pictures.

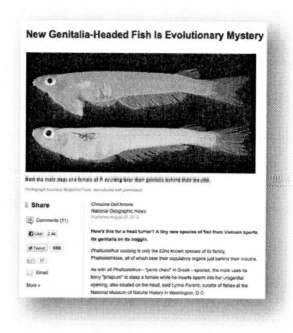

"I love those fish, Mommo," Marco said. "Can we get one?"

50.

A few weeks after the endoscopy, I made the mistake of planning a trip to New York City, in the middle of everything, to see my friend Cliff—stopping in Florida first to visit my parents—with Marco in tow, who at the time was three.

I was to take a red-eye, at that.

The first night at the airport, it was touch and go.

Marco had a cold and was cranky. His nose had been running all week. He had big red sores under his nostrils and was pretty miserable, especially five hours past his bedtime. But he looked up, sympathetically, from his stroller, and held my hand.

"Mommy's sick too," I told him. "We have to stay very quiet."

The plane was delayed—thunderstorms in New York. I had asked my new GP, Dr. Heng if he thought I was fit to fly. He said, "I don't see why not." My first visit, he had concluded that I was hypoglycemic and had sent me off with a glucometer and sugar tablets in case I felt like my blood sugar was getting low.

Lying across three seats at the gate, with Marco strapped into the stroller, his hand on my leg, I took sugar tabs every few minutes until I had downed them all. Pretty soon, I started to feel shaky. I tested my blood. My numbers were off the charts.

The wave of symptoms began to build. My hands had gone cold; I was weak; it was hard to breathe.

I put my head between my legs.

I looked around to see if there were paramedics nearby; it was an airport after all. There had to be people at the ready.

Maybe I should turn around and go home.

If I had been closer, I might have, but as it was, we had taken a taxi across the bridge to SFO to save money on the flight. My parents were awaiting me. Cliff had taken time off work for our visit.

I struggled through the days in Florida, trying not to let on. Many times I had to excuse myself, go into my room, and lie on the floor until I came to. Luckily, my parents nap a lot. There always seemed a moment when it was perfectly natural to lie down.

In Connecticut, visiting Cliff and his boyfriend, John, I felt so sick, I thought I would die. On Sunday, I called the Kaiser advice nurse.

But what could she do? Even in person, my condition was an enigma. It came and went. I seemed perfectly healthy. No one knew what to say.

I decided there was no point in staying any longer. For an extra three hundred bucks, I could leave the next day and be sick in the privacy of my own home.

So we got in the car and headed back to Cliff's apartment in New York.

It was eighty-seven degrees in Manhattan when we arrived at ten in the morning.

I told Cliff I needed more sugar tabs and had a very strong desire for protein. But, for some reason, during a moment of temporary respite, I decided to take Marco down the elevator in the stroller and walk the half block to the supermarket.

Twenty paces from Cliff's building, the symptoms overwhelmed me again. I knew for sure this time there was no turning back. I managed to call Cliff before I lay down on the ground, Marco in the stroller next to me.

In moments, Cliff was beside me. He led me back up to his apartment, where he called 911.

The men in blue took an inordinately long time to get there. I could hear Cliff beginning to lose it on the phone with the dispatcher. I lay on his bed, completely unable to speak. Marco curled himself around me.

"She's really sick. She's passing out. We need someone quick," Cliff said.

Finally—it must have been thirty minutes—six beefy New York City firemen carried me into the ambulance that was waiting for me downstairs. Cliff took Marco with him into the front. The guys hoisted me into the back and shut the door.

"Roosevelt Hospital or NYU?" they asked me.

"NYU," Cliff said, definitively. Then he turned to me. "It's a much better hospital."

I could have done a study of the emergency services of every major city in the country and across the world. I'd already been to the ER I-don't-know-how-many-times by the time I took this trip.

Once I was in the ambulance, they pumped me with bitingly cold oxygen and gunned the AC.

"How ya feelin? Miss Glancy," the paramedic by my side kept asking.

"I'm beginning to come back," I said. "I'm starting to come to."

Which was a good thing—because as it turned out, it was the worst possible day to pass out on New York City's West Side, if you wanted to be taken to a hospital on the East Side. We didn't realize it until we hit Fifth Avenue, but it was the day of the gay parade. That must have been why it had taken them so long to get to me. There were thousands, hundreds of thousands of half-naked, rainbow-flag-carrying gay people lining the streets. It had been maybe twenty-five years since I had been to the gay parade in New York City. I'm pretty sure the year Cliff's brother Ken died of AIDS, 1989, was the last time.

From inside the ambulance, it all looked like a blur. But most strange was the fact that I was almost entirely recovered. I felt a little weak, it's true, but the episode had passed.

Eventually, with a lot of honking and waving, the police actually stopped the parade for our ambulance so we could cross Fifth Avenue.

From the ambulance, I could hear the muffled sound of hundreds of gay baton twirlers belting out YMCA.

In a matter of minutes, we pulled into NYU Medical Center where I would chat up the interns, have yet another CT scan, and wait for hours to be released—just like back home. At least it was cool in there.

Sudha called on my cell phone while I was in the hospital. She was in Switzerland with Zane visiting her mother. We had a strained and difficult conversation, which was really the worst part of the whole experience. I had not yet come to understand how upset she was by what was happening with me, how it set off her deepest fears—and how in some part of herself, for fear she was losing me, she wanted to stop seeing me, to break up with me, and run away.

Marco and I left New York the next day. We had a brief layover during which I dragged Marco through the airport in search of a banana. I had run out of glucose tabs and thought I had to keep my blood sugar up (rather than down, as it would turn out), or I would again pass out. We found the banana and made it back to the plane on time.

But our brief layover was very sad—we lost Mickey Mouse in Denver.

51.

When I got home, I was utterly exhausted. I had been away from my computer for weeks. It seemed like a lot had gone down while I was gone. Occupy Oakland was still going strong. It was always good to see images of people fighting for the cause.

And then I saw an article that really disturbed me.

Attend Romney Event And
Lose Day's Pay

Songs, Now Charged
$675,000

Equal Access To Paralympics
Tickets

Former U.S. Poet Laureate Robert Hass Beaten At Occupy Berkeley

by Beth Buczynski | November 19, 2011 | 10:07 pm

Like   5,220 people like this. Be the first of your friends.

SHARE	5,220
TWEET	223
PIN IT	0
SHARE	104
COMMENT	276

I had vaguely heard this news when it was happening, but for some reason—I guess because I was underwater at the time—it had kind of gone by me.

How could anyone beat up Robert Hass?

Now here he was, looking very Bob. It has been years since I had even seen a picture of him.

52.

In 1997, the year I taught in Israel, Bob Hass was the keynote speaker at a conference I attended in Cairo. That year, I went to Cairo three times. For some reason, I felt strangely at home there.

I had met Bob for the first time at the Squaw Valley Writers Conference ten years earlier.

The Cairo conference was a bore. I ended up gambling in the hotel casino at night, smoking she-shah and exploring the city by day.

Bob's talk was on the last day. Probably there were two thousand people stuffed into a hot auditorium in the middle of Cairo in a neighborhood that bordered the Nile.

I have no memory of what his talk was about. I'm not sure I was listening very well either. I remember feeling distracted—by the excitement and the heat and the crowd—and perhaps by what was evoked by seeing him there. I do remember him reading his favorite poems aloud, however, and I was so moved to hear Dylan Thomas bellowed out in the middle of Cairo:

Now as I was young and easy
under the apple boughs
About the lilting house and happy as the grass was green,

The night above the dingle starry,

Time let me hail and climb . . .

When it was over, I debated about whether I should go up to the podium or not to say hello. It has been so long since I'd seen him. After much deliberation, I thought, what the hell.

"Gabby?"

"Hey, Bob!"

"What are you doing here?"

"I came to Cairo just to hear you talk!"

Bob laughed. I laughed. And then he motioned me to wait while other people approached him.

When the crowd finally calmed down, he came out from behind the podium.

"How long you here for?" he asked. He was looking at me sweetly, over the rims of his readers.

"I'm leaving tomorrow. How 'bout you?"

"Me, too," he said. "What are you doing here really?"

"I'm teaching in Israel."

"What are you doing for the rest of the day?"

"I was gonna go look for the only Jewish synagogue left standing in Cairo. It's kind of a crazy mission. I'm not even religious, but I think it would be an interesting thing to do."

"Can I come with you?" he said.

Bob Hass was chummy with my roommate at Squaw, Claudia Rankine, and it was originally through her that I had made a connection with him. But she and I had lost touch many years ago. I was really moved—and flattered—that he wanted to spend the day with me.

We hailed a cab from the lobby and asked the driver to take us to the Jewish synagogue. I had looked it up and it was about two and half miles from the hotel. By all accounts, it should have taken us about ten minutes, tops twenty, to get there.

In fact, it took us three hours. The streets were jammed up with donkey carts full of chickens and goats and sheep—and nothing was moving.

Our driver tried his best to take side streets, to maneuver around the carts, to do what he could to get us there.

There was squawking and mewling and baaing. Flies and dust and yelling.

Finally, in the late afternoon—it must have been about five by that time—we arrived at a dry grassy cemetery in the middle of nowhere. I had read that the Coptic cemetery was right next to the Jewish temple so I figured we were in the right place.

"Where's the temple?" Bob asked the driver.

The driver pointed to a patch of dry grass across the road that was in front of what was a very spotty cemetery—there were maybe twenty-five graves.

Bob and I looked at each other. It had taken us so long to get here. It was late and we were tired.

The driver came out of the car and opened the door for us. He pointed again to the patch of grass. We paid him. We looked around—and at each other.

"Where the hell are we?"

We laughed.

Perhaps the synagogue was on the other side of the cemetery?

We walked through it. Wind in dry weeds was the only sound.

We talked easily. We walked in circles, talking.

Finally we saw some other tourists.

"We're looking for the synagogue," Bob called out. "Do you know where we might find it?"

The tourists, who turned out to be Australian, said you had to go underground to get to the other side of this dry river bed—and there we would find it.

So Bob and I went underground. The dry clotted dirt opened up just to the other side of the cemetery where we had come in—and ahead of us there were stairs.

Again, we looked at each other. What a day it had been already. But why turn back now?

So Bob went first and I followed. It was a cool, damp tunnel underground, also dirt, that gave onto some stairs about twenty paces to the other side.

We climbed the stairs and there before us—as if in a dream—was a big black door to nowhere. It had a frame but was not connected to any building.

"This is the synagogue?" I turned to Bob.

It was.

Again, we laughed. It was funny to have driven so far to see this. It was funny and sad at the same time—because this was all that was left of the only Jewish synagogue in Cairo.

Dusk was upon us. We realized that we had no idea where we were or how we would get back.

We had not seen another cab since we had been dropped off here. It didn't seem like a place anyone would come.

Suddenly, out of nowhere, a cab arrived.

Wildly, we hailed it—although we were the only ones there.

It was the same driver. He must have realized we would need a ride back.

Otherwise, I'm not sure how we would ever have gotten back to our hotel.

The way back took just as long as the way there. The loudspeakers bellowed out that droning chant I had come to love, the call to prayer. The traffic once again was at a near standstill.

But this time, the carts were stacked with carcasses—the skins of the goats and sheep we had seen on the way there—and there was blood running down all the streets and clouds of flies buzzing around the carts and the strong smell of burning meat in the dusty twilight air.

We had had no idea it was the Festival of the Slaughter—a holy day in the middle of spring.

But there it was.

Back at the hotel, we had a late dinner at the restaurant, which was almost closing. Then Bob asked if I wanted to have coffee with him at the café, which was open till eleven. Neither of us wanted to part. It was something about what we had witnessed together. It was spooky and surreal and beautiful all at once—and it was as if it would turn into a dream once we were alone with it.

Just before we went to our separate rooms, Bob asked, "What are you writing these days?"

I suddenly got shy.

"I saw your poem in *The New Yorker*," he said. "Have you published any books?

I shook my head.

At that moment, he took out his card, turned it over and wrote the address of his country house in Inverness, California, on the back and said, looking into my eyes, and putting his hand on my shoulder, "Call me, Gabby. I'd love to help you in any way I can."

Bob Hass was Poet Laureate of the United States at that time. I was moved and flattered and thanked him for the offer and for coming with me on our pilgrimage.

I never called him.

I misplaced his card, in fact, and only found it many years later tucked away in a Fossil watch tin shaped like a Band-Aid box. I had had three or four miscarriages by then. Perhaps it was after I lost the twins. In my despair, I had gone to a support group for women who had miscarried at all stages along the way. Someone in the group had suggested I start a "God Box," into which I could put my dreams for the future, even the name of my babies-to-be, written on folded up pieces of paper, in hopes my dreams would someday come true. It seemed like a way to keep the dream alive of having a baby without having to worry about it every day.

I was looking for the perfect "God Box" when I found the Fossil tin —and in it, I found the card Bob had given me that day.

Even then, I didn't call him.

That I rediscovered Bob's card in my God Box-to-be seemed auspicious, however—for one dream or the other—and it made me laugh. I was relieved to find it, just in case I should ever want to call him, although—and I felt some sadness thinking about it—I might have missed my chance.

The feeling lasted only a split second, however.

The next moment, I put my little folded-up piece of paper in my God Box, held it up to the heavens, and speaking to the powers that be, said something like: "Here! I'm giving this to you. You take it and do what you will with it."

I left Bob's card in the box. I figured, why not, it was already in there. Maybe one day, I could hope for that too.

For the moment, though, all I wanted was a baby.

When I returned to Israel after that trip to Cairo, I was violently ill. I think I can trace that case of parasites back to the sausage pizza I ate at the Khan El Khalili bazaar. Even at the time, I thought, "Isn't this what Cliff ate when he got sick? This is probably not a good idea."

Thankfully, the doctors in Israel know how to treat Egyptian parasites. In fact, I'm sure it's the best place in the world to be treated for such a thing. In two weeks, I was up and running, though my stomach was a little worse for wear.

That night, the night I ate Egyptian sausage pizza, weaving through throngs of tourists and Egyptian men—the women were all indoors—I got lost. I had taken a wrong turn and found myself in a narrow alley, alone. All the sudden, seemingly out of nowhere, I was surrounded by a group of Egyptian boys—maybe there were six or eight of them—in their late teens. I wasn't sure what was happening.

What could they possibly want with me?

I was just about to get scared when the last call to prayer of the day sounded out of the loudspeakers above our heads, and, through the open door of an inconspicuous mosque we happened to be in front of, I caught sight of a hundred men falling to their knees.

The boys dispersed as suddenly as they had come together—and I flew out of an opening in the circle that had surrounded me and off to find my way back to the bazaar.

That was the night before I met Bob. I even told him about it—pizza and all—on our walk through the Coptic cemetery.

I am remembering now that the plane back to Tel Aviv was delayed. We had boarded and then had to deplane because there was suspicion of a bomb. In Israel, if you leave your groceries unattended for even five minutes, they block off the street and explode the bag into a million pieces. It's crazy over there. And, as I mentioned before, the El Al security people are ruthless. Don't ever flirt with those guys. They'll detain you in the airport for hours.

Ours was a night flight—only two hours to Israel—that would not leave until seven a.m. the next morning.

The Israelis on that particular plane were either kibbutzim— they looked like hippies—or guys and girls in the army. Either way, they knew what to do in situations like this: Go to sleep.

So we all bedded down—using our backpacks as pillows— and curled up on the floor or on the empty seats in the otherwise completely deserted Cairo airport.

Beside me that night was, of all people, Jane Goodall, the famous anthropologist. She had also been at the conference the day before to give a talk on the emotional life of chimpanzees.

She was near seventy at the time, slim and fit, with long gray hair and beautiful smooth brown skin. She was wearing a white linen shirt that came down to her knees, baggy powder-blue lin- en trousers and sandals. She looked like she was right off the veld.

We slept two feet from each other.

I knew who she was but I didn't talk to her.

53.

Frustrated, desperate, sicker than ever, I once again texted Caitlin.

Chew didn't work out. Can't seem to diagnose problem. Got anyone else?

Caitlin said her avenue of last resort finally did the trick. She passed the name of her integrative medicine guru, Chris Kresser, on to me. For that, I will be forever grateful.

Chris Kresser took a very thorough medical history from me. In fact, in order to see him, you have to write it yourself. Mine was ten pages long.

Within minutes of looking at me, Chris Kresser asked me if, in all my medical travels, I had had a stool test.

"Nope," I said. "Not one."

"We'll do a test to be sure, but it seems like a no-brainer to me. In the meantime, go on the caveman diet. Whatever you've got, it'll be good for you."

And so I went home, pooped into a red-and-white-striped paper french fry tray—that's what they provide you in the kit—mixed my poop into special vials—three kinds of poisonous solutions—shook each one for thirty seconds—and Fedexed the whole package to a lab in Duluth, Georgia.

Three weeks and a mere two hundred dollars later, I was diagnosed with a raging case of *Strongyloides* (a potentially fatal parasite, as its name suggests), *Trichuria trichosis* (pinworms, which I had most likely gotten and not fully gotten rid of in Cairo), and *Morganella morganii* (an opportunistic bacteria I may have picked up in the ER).

I can only imagine I picked up the *Strongyloides*, a parasite found in Central and South America, on one of my many trips to visit Marco in Guatemala before the adoption was complete.

It was a relief to finally get a diagnosis. All this time something *had* been eating me from the inside. That's certainly what it felt like.

I wish I could say I was immediately cured. As it turned out, the parasites were almost as difficult to treat as they were to diagnose.

Four courses of Ivermectin and Mebendazole (human DDT) later, my stomach was ripped to shreds on the inside, where the worms had bedded down, and is still in the process of healing.

Nonetheless, things started looking up once the parasites were under control. Slowly, I began to feel better. Two days would go by without a faint. I started walking—first to the end of the block, then to the creek near my house. I no longer dreaded going to work. I began to trust I could make it there and back—and survive. Instead of avoiding Marco and Zane, I actually found myself wanting to play with them.

One day I decided I should try to explain to them what had happened.

"Mommo's had worms," I said. The boys were four and five years old by this time.

"Worms?"

"Yup," I said. "Eating my stomach!"

They looked at me amazed.

I drew a picture of an oval with little yellow squiggles inside. "That's my stomach. And those are the worms."

They seemed to find the whole thing very amusing. For weeks, they asked me to tell them the same story again and again.

Within a few months, Sudha and I decided to move in together. I guess she began to believe I wasn't just about to die. In fact, we decided to buy a house. Suddenly it seemed there was hope.

I have Chris Kresser to thank for this. I'm glad someone finally suggested I take a look at my shit.

54.

Sudha and I are lying under the shade of an old mulberry tree, a throwback to my childhood in Brooklyn. The leaves are just on the turn, quivering in the light wind of an October afternoon. We place our blanket down in the halo of black-red berries that have long since dried and put our shoes on each corner of the blanket to hold it down.

Sudha had taken the day off to renew Zane's Swiss passport, the kids are in school—they just started kindergarten and first grade. Sudha and I have a rare moment in the middle of the day, just us.

The weather is unseasonably warm. Indian summer. And we decide to lie down in our own backyard. This time, for once, it's not because I'm just about to pass out.

When the tree was in full leaf, not that many months ago, I remember one day sitting on the porch looking at it through the haze of a moment in which I could barely see through my eyes. The light must have been just right that day because out of nowhere, now and again, I caught sight of an inchworm, its tiny green see-through body, swinging in and out of the light on its own gossamer thread.

Of course, at the time, I thought perhaps I might have been seeing things.

Now here we are so many months later.

Looking at the sky through the quivering green web of leaves over our heads, we are contemplating life's mysteries.

"Sometimes it's hard to have a body, isn't it?" Sudha says to me.

For a moment, I have no idea what she means.

I look at the tree, the sky, the hills behind our house. In one of my hands, I feel blades of cool grass, Sudha's hand in my other. I think about Marco and his firm brown arms and legs, my aged parents, their bodies growing more and more frail.

"I guess so," I said. "But is there life without a body?"

Just then, dimly but distinctly in the background, we hear the patterned chirping of the White-breasted nuthatch emanating from the kitchen where we hung the singing bird clock my parents gave us for Christmas.

For a moment we are silent.

Every hour the clock sings the song of a different bird—tufted titmouse, black-capped chickadee, white-throated sparrow. Whenever it sounds, we pause to listen to it—a voice from another world. Sometimes the real birds in our backyard actually respond with a song of their own.

"Is there life without a body?" Sudha repeats my question wistfully when the singing ceases. "Of course there is!" she says, as if it's the most obvious thing in the world.

55.

But actually it's not obvious at all.

In fact, it is as subtle and ubiquitous as all the microorganisms that make up the being-field we call the self.

Beyond the poetic resonances and spiritual implications of such a moment in the grass with my beloved lies a very strange coincidence.

While we were lying under the mulberry tree contemplating the cosmos, Facebook friend and literary agent Holly Bemiss, whose protobacteria must have intuited mine, posted this link to an article by Michael Pollan on my timeline.

According to Pollan:

"It turns out that we are only 10 percent human: for every human cell that is intrinsic to our body, there are about 10 resident microbes — including commensals (generally harmless freeloaders) and mutualists (favor traders) and, in only a tiny number of cases, pathogens. To the extent that we are bearers of genetic information, more than 99 percent of it is microbial. And it appears increasingly likely that this "second genome," as it is sometimes called, exerts an influence on our health as great and possibly even greater than the genes we inherit from our parents."

Without knowing it, perhaps this is what Sudha was trying to say. There is life beyond what we know as our bodies. And what we think of as self goes far beyond the boundaries of our skin.

10 percent human and 90 percent bugs? Perhaps it's our bugs that fell in love.

We used to think the immune system had this fairly straightforward job," Michael Fischbach, a biochemist at the University of California, San Francisco, says. "All bacteria were clearly 'nonself' so simply had to be recognized and dealt with. But the job of the immune system now appears to be far more nuanced and complex. It has to learn to consider our mutualists (e.g., resident bacteria) as self too. In the future we won't even call it the immune system, but the microbial interaction system. The absence of constructive engagement between microbes and immune system (particularly during certain windows of development) could be behind the increase in autoimmune conditions in the West.

—Michael Pollan, "Some of My Best Friends are Germs," The New York Times, May 15, 2013

It's something to think about all right, how what comes out the back of your car erodes not only the atmosphere but the lining of your stomach, causing the near extinction of the teeming rainforest of microbiota that has long since kept the human creature safe.

56.

When I was about ninety percent recovered, Chris said I could add a small amount of dark chocolate back into my diet. This may not seem significant, but it was revolutionary. Although I had all intentions of starting slow, once I started, I couldn't stop. The chocolate made me completely high. The trees seemed to speak to me, their leaves so much greener and pointier than I remembered. At moments, I heard Tibetan monks chanting in the wind. Life seemed to speed up and slow down at the same time. In fact, I began having the visions that led to this book.

57.

When you're sick, you think it's never going to end. You've always been sick, and you always will be. When you're well, it's hard to remember there was ever anything wrong with you. Although it took me a long time to recover—which ultimately meant balancing the good worms with the bad—eventually I traded in my sick passport and re-entered the kingdom of the (mostly) well.

As my life force increased, so my appetite for the "microbial interaction system" that is Facebook all but fell away. In fact, I would have to say I almost developed an aversion to it. I guess I came to associate Facebook with that awful feeling I could never identify— the feeling of being eaten alive.

Then one day, August 10, 2012, in a moment of idle curiosity, I decided once again to smell the trees. It had been many months since I had done so.

There I came upon the very sad news that my old friend David Rakoff, one of the most brilliant writers and kindest men I ever knew, died of cancer. I had known he was sick. Cliff had, in fact, warned me that probably any day now he would die.

But it was through Facebook that I first heard the news.

It's a weird way to find out someone has died.

Word travels fast on Facebook—in a way—though weeks after David's death, I continued to receive notices such as this:

Nevertheless, I found myself, once again, completely consumed, recording image after image, pages and pages of screen shots.

And then it happened. Sad, obsessed, haunted by images of David's life, suddenly, out of the blue, I found the image I had lost so many months ago. I couldn't believe it.

Seeing it recalled to me that awful night after the endoscopy when I had seen and, inexplicably lost, the image in the first place.

For a moment, I sit back in my chair and fill the self that is sitting there with my own awareness and pleasure, as if I were a whole universe awake to its own existence.

I am simultaneously sad and happy and moved.

Unlike David, I have survived this journey and, finally, am lucky enough to be alive and awake all at the same time.

Being—and life itself, I find myself thinking, *it's there for a moment . . .*

And then *poof.*

58.

But not without one last hurrah.

Appearing before me, as vivid as daylight, there again is David—reincarnated on Facebook, again, and once again.

This time in a tuxedo, debonair as ever, grinning devilishly, as if to say, *More to the point, the trick is on you . . .*

.

59.

Recently, I read an article in which a new-age doctor said the first question he asks patients is "What do YOU think is wrong with you?"

I wish someone had asked me that question. I would have told them what I did tell them. Something is eating me.

60.

"That's it?" Sudha turns to me. "That's where it ends?"

"What do you mean?" I say. "You know the story. Isn't that what happened?"

"You didn't tell them about the murders. It's not every day there's a double homicide in front of your house, and you have to move out of it because you think the guy who did it lives next door?"

"That's true," I said, "but I'm saving that for the next book."

"I don't know." She is shaking her head.

I can see she's afraid to upset me.

"I just don't think it's finished, honey," she says. "It needs something . . . maybe something spiritual?"

"The whole thing is spiritual!" I say to her.

Now I am really getting annoyed.

"Something political, maybe, political *and* spiritual," she says. "I don't know. I just feel something is missing."

We are in bed after a long day, Sudha's MacBook Air propped up on a pillow between us. While I read her the ending I had just written, Osho appears on the computer screen, sitting in a big chair—black robes, white beard—spouting decrees like

173

God on judgment day. Kimmie, her friend from India, has posted a link to *Osho, Spiritual Terrorist* on Sudha's timeline.

"There I am," Sudha says suddenly, pointing to the screen. She thinks she sees herself among the thousands of hippie *sanyassins* dressed in orange, bowing in prayer.

"The moment has come for the new man to arise," Osho is saying. "Otherwise there will be nothing left—not. even. one. single. wild. flower."

"Can we turn that down?" I say.

"Sure, honey, sorry." Sudha says, "I got distracted."

I am disturbed. Mostly because I think Sudha is right—and I'm afraid I won't be able to locate what is missing.

I can feel I am a breath away from turning what has been a lovely evening into a disaster.

To her credit, Sudha reaches across the keyboard and takes my hand.

For a moment, we sit in silence.

Then she pipes up. "I've got it," she says. "It needs questions at the end, something that makes people think about how all this stuff you've written about you has to do with them."

61.

So why haven't we evolved our own systems to perform these most critical functions of life? Why have we outsourced all this work to a bunch of microbes? One theory is that, because microbes evolve so much faster than we do (in some cases a new generation every 20 minutes), they can respond to changes in the environment — to threats as well as opportunities — with much greater speed and agility than 'we' can.

"This plasticity serves to extend our comparatively rigid genome, giving us access to a tremendous bag of biochemical tricks we did not need to evolve ourselves. The bacteria in your gut are . . . a microbial mirror of the changing world. And because they can evolve so quickly, they help our bodies respond to changes in our environment.

—Michael Pollan, "Some of My Best Friends are Germs," The New York Times, May 15, 2013

That's beautiful, I think. *Such a perfect solution.*

But what happens when the balance is disrupted?

At the gym today, while spinning away on my stationary bike, I caught sight of a story about a woman, a very pretty forty-something Mom—shiny dark hair, beautiful eyes—from Arizona—accused of smuggling marijuana in Mexico.

She was traveling by bus to a family funeral when twelve pounds of weed was found under her seat. Images of her and her husband—a handsome, clean-cut guy with blue eyes—and of the road to the Mexican jail where she has been for almost a week—appeared over and over on the screen.

What if that were me? I began to think.

In fact, it could be me.

At the end of the month, we are taking a long-awaited family holiday to Cabo. It will be the first time I will have left the country since I adopted Marco from Guatemala.

For a moment, it all becomes too vivid.

I see myself languishing in a Mexican prison, unable to digest whatever food I am given without my *Saccharomyces boulardii* and VSL #3, the most potent probiotic formula known to man (not to mention, I'm gluten free!).

Surely, I would die. If I even miss a dose, my stomach starts to blow up and things start getting weird.

Luckily, technology has evolved—rapidly enough, in my case—to keep up with the evolution—or extinction, as it were—of my essential bugs. The truth is at this point in my life, my microbiome can no longer exist without help.

What happened? What caused the balance in me to shift so dramatically?

Too much fun in my twenties? All the hormones I took to try to have a child? All those miscarriages late in life. Two courses of arythromyacin following a tooth extraction? Anorexia in my youth? Chemtrails? Genetic modification? Global warming? I don't even like to think about it.

There is no escaping how precarious the situation really is—for my own uncharted interior wilderness, as well as for the planet.

> A handful of microbiologists have begun sounding the alarm about our civilization's unwitting destruction of the human microbiome and its consequences. Important microbial species may have already gone extinct, before we have had a chance to learn who they are or what they do. What we think of as an interior wilderness may, in fact, be nothing of the kind, having long ago been reshaped by unconscious human actions.
>
> —Michael Pollan, "Some of My Best Friends are Germs," The New York Times, May 15, 2013

Whatever it is, it is disturbing.

Is it reversible? Is there any way to turn back the clock? Will the pathogens win?

Perhaps mine have brought me to my conclusion.

Amidst the love and the wildflowers, the flotsam and jetsam of what gets tossed "randomly" out of the social biosphere into my soul, I rather think this particular journey should end with the title of Facebook friend Rachel Livitsky's book: *The Story of My Accident is Ours.*

Acknowledgements

For her patience when I could do nothing more than eat almonds, drink salt water and facebook, I'd like to thank my partner, Sudha Faraday. Thank you also for believing I would eventually get better even when I lost hope—and for pressing me to find the ending for this book that was just right.

Thanks to my sons, Marco and Zane, for loving me through the rough times.

Thanks to Clifford Chase for reminding me of who I was before I got sick and for having faith I would get back to myself —and for his invaluable insight and attention to detail in reading and rereading drafts.

Thanks to the many people who helped along the way including Dr. Alex Zaphiris, Peter Koshland, Tracy Atkins, Laura Duffy, Laura Jacoby, Bob Croslin, David Rakoff, Eileen Myles, Robert Haas, Caitlin Sislin, Holly Bemiss and Meg Allen—and all those who gave me permission to use their Facebook posts and/or photos.

Special thanks to Chris Kresser for his ability to see the obvious and find ways to meet it.

To all the nurses, firefighters, paramedics and technicians I met in the course of this journey -- thank you for your kindness and friendship.

To the doctors, trapped in the system, who tried to diagnose me—I couldn't have written this book without you.

To my parents for their unwavering support—on this project, and always.

And thanks to Margaret Crastnopol, ever my muse.

About Gabrielle Glancy

Winner of a New York Foundation for the Arts Fellowship in Fiction, a Writers at Work Prize and the Malinche Prize for her translation of the acclaimed French writer, Marguerite Duras, Gabrielle Glancy has published fiction and poetry in *The New Yorker*, *The Paris Review*, *The American Poetry Review* and many other journals and anthologies. She is the author of *The Art of the College Essay* and Series Editor of *Best College Essays*. A college admissions expert, she is one of the foremost professionals in her field. She lives in Oakland, California with her partner and two sons.